Tequila Sunrise
for Business

The awaken of the force

Acnowledgments

To each and every one of the people who with their intention no matter what it was, helped to get this project.

Dedications

To my beloved daughters: Alanna & Astrid Flores, the most valuable beings in my life. Their mere existence illuminates my path.

Only through the true unity of all can we create a reality parallel to the system, since we are one triple energy and project it

ARTIUX

Content

Tequila Sunrise
for Business

Introduction
The intention of this cocktail

The only way to do great work is to love what you do
STEVE JOBS
American entrepreneur, marketer and inventor

The metaphorical combination of this book represents only a simple form the basis on which the power of life is expressed to create reality in business. In its ancestral ingredients that exist in all the parts and it is possible to recognize, it is encrypted the formula that by analogy I have called Tequila Sunrise for its easy assimilation. By its nature, the strength of these ingredients has been incorporated in the largest companies throughout history demonstrating to keep the system active successfully. And I have concentrated them here so that you learn to delight them. So that you learn to master in the Matrix. While you are inside it and it subsists.

Tequila Sunrise aims you make yours the infusion of fundamentals, develops its processes and recognizes the vehicles that are proper to these three ingredients. That you adopt the positive way of being inside to create a reality parallel to the system.

The ingredients that represents to the Tequila Sunrise on business have evolved with a particular purpose, get everything that every big successful company has wanted to get, money. And they have had a common sense, because well combined have shown to form a great power that works effectively to succeed in what we call business.

For they represent the foundations that: one, move business in general in the current commercial system. And here I tell you clearly: two, you will know to perform your projects in particular that you consistently want to achieve.

In the process of serving the three ingredients that shape the Tequila Sunrise for Business, it must take into account the importance and function that takes the ice cubes as the basis of the cocktail ingredients, that every enterprise must know pouring into your business as a catalyst, to understand how its freezing temperature develops best qualities to the objective you want to see reflected in material reality; thus giving temper to the mix.

This cold ingredient emphasizes its action since: The beginning of the elaboration: to be planted with the solid presence that will act in the ingredients. During preparation: to maintain the important temperature required for the cocktail. And until the end of the tasting: to obtain the expected results it produces its effect.

That is, throughout the realization of any business project, by the fact that it achieves the desired effect only by impregnating its cold temperature in the three ingredients of the cocktail and when these are poured into it in the correct order as here is posed.

And it is along the preparation of the cocktail, that the ice cubes is developing its characteristic qualities in its most pure expression. Qualities that must be present and must act to correctly precise all business movements, they indicate how to let at their best the delicate preparation of Tequila Sunrise for Business. And you will glimpsing on in each ingredient.

Likewise, you will learn from some points of view of several authors, specific studies on these main ingredients used in business, and the most outstanding rules that have followed some of the most important businessmen. Rules that have led them to get the success in their business. By supporting you in diagrams that will help you to learn.

For finally, you realize that the correct preparation of this combined elixir in your business causes a unique effect, that from the mind of your company rises to that of your consumer like the Sunrise Effect.

And once there, allow yourself to understand how to drive the direction of business that you want, so that from now on, those around you and the consumer learn to distinguish the moments when this effect goes up their mind in such a way that causes them win in their life and you in business.

It depends heavily on the correct combination of Tequila Sunrise for Business, so that your firm is well endowed with all its qualities and that one to one conformed in your projects and thus you can achieve with them the effect they need, since only with the will to go for what you want you can get the preparation, revelation, and the result you require in your business.

That is, when you reach the complete visualization of how to configure your company, one, you will understand how to develop your projects; two, you will control how to position a product properly; and three, you will notice the effect that Tequila Sunrise for Business can have when it rises in the mind and influences in the decision of purchase of the consumer, by acting promptly in the decisive moments in which your projects and your business they are followed by many people. For now in general, you correctly achieve your major business objectives. Seeing thus their material results as a consequence of success and earn what you want to achieve.

The overall objective of Tequila Sunrise for Business is that you develop fully their ingredients interleaved by the ice necessary, in order to strengthen your company, you get success in your business, and you obtain better results in your life; and together related to a global fact: to dominate in the Matrix with the Sunrise.

Knowing the legend

Get excited and enthusiastic about you own dream, this excitement is like a forest fire, you can smell it, taste it, and see it from a mile away
DENIS WAITLEY
American motivational speaker and writer, consultant, and best-selling author

One of the secrets it holds life within each of the entities it creates, is clearly marked in a cocktail that is well known by all; of course I mean the Tequila Sunrise. This drink keeps visibly defined its special combination, and into the quality of each of its ingredients, by the combined effect, they are accurately reflected the functions it has to play any company to achieve success.

The presence of tequila goes from tradition to the law by the time of the Mexican Revolution when Porfirio Diaz organized to promote the drink called "mezcal wine" at a fair in San Antonio Texas to that in that place they called wine tequila for the location which came.

There are references since 1943 to protect the name "tequila" and to obtain the exclusivity of use, focusing on a long history associated with the region's industry, the town and the hill with this drink. Since 1958, Mexico protected designations of origin and their international registration.

Designation of Origin (DO) is the name of a geographical region that serves to designate a product originating therein and whose quality or characteristics are due exclusively to the geographical environment. Products with designation of origin in the world cannot be produced in any more side than its original place. Worldwide, only 187 municipalities in five states in Mexico are allowed and can produce tequila. Designation of Origin Tequila (DOT) comprises all municipalities Jalisco and some of Michoacan, Nayarit, Guanajuato and Tamaulipas. This means that all drinks called tequila, both in Mexico and abroad, should come from factories in this region, under the supervision of the *Consejo Regulador del Tequila (CRT)* [Tequila Regulatory Council]. So no one can use the Designation of Origin Tequila, which is the word tequila, to distinguish any product, if not authorized by the Mexican government, through the institution designated to protect it, which in this case is the CRT.

Mexico has the Designation of Origin Tequila, and it is considered the national drink.

The tequila industry is seeking exclusive use of the word agave for tequila in their bottles. This means excluding others that sell industrial products with the same raw material. Therefore argue that exist in the market beverages even when made from the agave plant are not only distilled entirely made with blue variety *wever* kind *tequilana*. The consumer buys drinks thinking it's a real blue agave tequila, without being so.

Note that to this effort also meet producers of other non-generic or distilled beverages, which are also made with agave. In the case of *mezcal* and *bacanora*, they also are affected by brands that use reputation built for these products.

Therefore we must know the different kinds of tequila that are five and a go from low to high maturity: white, young, rested, aged and extra aged.

And to be considered 100 percent agave must be of a single species of this plant without mixing with other species of agave.

The tequila houses and its more than 200 years of tradition reinforce its presence to see consolidated its recognition in the international market.

Already for the sixties tequila it is relatively famous in the world and especially in some countries like Japan and Spain. Since 1973 the General Declaration of Protection of the Designation of Origin "Tequila" is requested. An agreement between Mexico and the US establishes by which Mexico agrees in preventing the use of the name "Bourbon" within its territory and the US public the recognition to Tequila as a distinctive and exclusive product of Mexico in the Federal Register. In 1974 Canada restricts the use of Tequila name to products from Mexico, and the Mexican government granted the protection to the Designation of Origin Tequila. In 1977 the territory of Designation of Origin is extended to some municipalities of Tamaulipas.

In 1978 the certificate of registration of Tequila is obtained in the "Registre International des Appelations D'origine" of the World Intellectual Property Organization (Geneva, Switzerland). In 1981 the Province of Quebec (Canada) expressed appreciation to the DOT. Denmark in 1982 recognizes the DOT but it has taken years recognition from other countries. In Russia is obtained in 2012.

Today, tequila has one of the highest standards of quality and prestige. And it certainly ranks as one of the most recognized beverages produced in Mexico and sold around the world. The history of tequila and their houses are closely related, as their tequila dynasties are so old that today, this famous liqueur, is one of the most grounded in the Mexican and international markets.

The market for tequila in Mexico is on the Tequila region par excellence which is el Bajio, however the heartland concentrates largely in consumption by population density. Approximately 60 percent of consumers in Mexico prefer to take it as tequila cocktail Paloma. Approximately 100 000 Palomas are consumed per hour.

America is the country's best-selling tequila over Mexico with an approximate consumption of 11 million boxes. Higher consumption is generated in USA through the cocktail Margarita, with approximately 200 000 Margaritas per hour consumed.

Tequila is one of the best cards of Mexico in the world and its unique flavor is increasingly sought in international markets. (*Revistafortuna; Consejo Regulador del Tequila*, 2013)

Tequila Sunrise was coined by Gene Sulit, a former employee who worked at the Arizona Biltmore Hotel by various occupations between the decades 1930 and 1940, during his time as a bartender, after one of his regular customers asked for a cocktail, combining his love for the Tequila with his preference for taste drinks poolside. The story can be found in detail in the resort's Wright bar. (Phoenixnewtimes, 2015)

Tequila Sunrise which was created and served for the first time originally contained (tequila, crème de cassis, lemon juice and soda water).

The modern Tequila Sunrise is a cocktail made of tequila, orange juice, and grenadine syrup and served unmixed in a tall glass with ice cubes.

This drink was originated from California in the early 1970s and was created by Bobby Lazoff and Billy Rice while working as young bartenders at the Trident in Sausalito, California north of San Francisco.

The cocktail is named for its appearance when served, with gradations of color resembling a sunrise.

And here is contained the relation that this one cocktail has with business, it is in evolution; once obtained, it is very important to achieve the characteristic flavor and effect of Tequila Sunrise, by activating the combined power that their ingredients have. Evolution that in a company, is the result of achieving the differentiation, the leadership and financial independence, present to properly activate their ingredients through the role of its organs, which have aim to develop the combination of their qualities secret to obtain the Sunrise on your business.

In 1972, at a private party at the Trident organized by Bill Graham to kick off the Rolling Stones' 1972 tour in America, Mick Jagger had one of the cocktails, liked it, and he and his entourage started drinking them down. They later ordered them all across America, even dubbing the tour itself their "cocaine and tequila sunrise tour." (Wikipedia.org, 2015). In my opinion, that decision changed the reality and manifests something unique.

From this success is treated, to have the decision to achieve a goal with the intention of creating a new reality, than with determination is so different, that is made special.

Of the Tequila Sunrise for Business

My biggest motivation? Just to keep challenging myself
RICHARD BRANSON
English businessman and investor

Mexico City. 1999. Two years after college. Professor of design business, the sun rises, the party abounds, the Matrix catches, businesses captivate, and however … life is creating … Noting the potential: Let us raise the sun and we reflect life.

Full time, high passion, little gains. I got married. Looking for better opportunities I changed of work. Some old acquaintances who 8 years ago they asked me I gift them a drawing of mine as a personal present, which I found to be flattering even though they did not give me something in return, they searched me again offering me a place. Welcome Yucatan, the deal was, you work for us, rickety salary but live surrounded by peace a heavenly place, and eventually, you go releasing alone. But, a detail emerged, I was their marketing designer 'for great things' as they defined it and, they closed me the doors to the study of the preferences and consumer's profile, and trends of market competition? I had a talk with some of his employees to make a new design, when I saw that drawing they asked me gifted printed on t-shirts, and then they told me everything. That old acquaintances had already won thousands with the drawing, which immediately was a success for them for several years without comment me a word, and when that goldmine were exhausted, they looked at me again. That's not honest. Do they only want to squeeze me? If they were to succeed, it does not work. On the other hand, that was not the deal. Neither would be fulfilled with his type of dealings. Or perhaps, they saw me as their own competition? All that spun around and back to Mexico City as a teacher, teaching staff was reduced and I'm out of work. Mistakes committed? No. Unforgettable apprenticeships. In the pursuit of success few people are on your side, although on your unfavorable conditions, it may be that even your nearest hesitate, distrust, and changes of opinion about you as soon as possible. Others simply see you as an obstacle. And there are those who know your talent and therefore ignore you, or you are not seen with good eyes. Looking for work and being ignored. Time goes by. I was having all the enthusiasm in contributing my knowledge to bear fruit with a company. But the same is repeated. Rejected requests. Again and again. A true crossing.

In 2007 after having traveled endless vacancies, to be welcomed by a couple of fruit of half time and little juice, no home, and with two beautiful daughters; when I began my research undergraduate thesis in graphic design, I decided to conduct a study to some design companies. So, not only it would provide good experiences about design on the business context, but also that study would serve as a basis to later elucidate how the energy of life is expressed to create reality in business. How their three forces are indispensable in every size of business as ingredients. And how do they require them to work in unison and combine well, to provoke success in business.

To apply this study first I sent the documents by e-mail to Antonio Perez Iragorri director of the, *a! Diseño* magazine; after whom I contacted by phone and I described the project that I called: "Design Management in Design Companies of Mexico City" for permission to query information from various copies of his magazines quoting reference. I said, "The intent is to demonstrate the importance of design in business, and also, that acts alongside two other disciplines, all three are of utmost importance when doing business." He kindly agreed and had an immediate positive response to the project. He replied, "I like your interest in business, you can take the information you need."

My goal was to interview twelve design offices. Throughout the study requested collaboration thirty-two design companies, it was a labor of much insistence that lasted months. To each I sent by e-mail the information from the interview that apply, with my academic identification from *Universidad Nacional Autónoma de México (UNAM)* [National Autonomous University of Mexico], my address and local telephone. After one or two hours, I contacted them by phone again to make the invitation to participate in the study and explain the intent of this. I was instructed that they would pass information and I to call two to three days after. I called each company the day indicated to ask if they agreed and if so, arrange an appointment. Twenty-four offices agreed to analyze information therefore with them I should be not only persistent but convincing and achieve my goal.

To achieve the visit I said, "You are the main companies that know how to lead the successful of a design project. Your designs are all over the country and many of them reach several Latin America and the United States, why you would not give back with their knowledge to the profession?" After a grueling monitoring them, only twelve began the process of visit. Was not possible! 'The Achilles heel' of design is its lack of interest by the vast majority of any type of companies and the reaction of the design companies to a project, which in theory would work to their recognition in business was not what one would expect from those who care about the business of his profession.

In spite of being planted on several occasions I kept insisting depth. I got that eight of the thirty-two companies agree to be interviewed. I made sure to adapt to your time for their convenience. I applied the interviews each company as they were doing me a space on their agenda. At the agreed places I took the printed interview to read the questions and then write down the answers.

Five of them were visited in their offices, three answered the interview by e-mail, and one for conversation phone call. There was no important office that would continue the process, and I had to get my goal, so I took the support of Mr. Iragorri getting the information of some of its magazine copies, for the three missing offices. The study ended until I met up with the full information. Two years. It was an arduous work.

Just after my divorce, I graduated.

In 2010, I met a former commercial director of one of Grupo Carso's companies, Pedro Jaime Ochoa, who started his own business and from whom I learned the basis of the MLM through his lectures. And that was the point where it was clear to me. Business had already achieved an important advance to take a new course within the Matrix, had expressed its evolution. By knowing the network marketing I realized that in business had already developed the creative energy of nature with the formula that envisioned financial freedom, which would push companies have to adopt this way of doing business for not to stay in the way. And all this strongly supported how I noticed and could feel that the energy of nature is expressed as three ingredients to at some point take evolution and create reality in this case in business.

However, employed as an 'intermittent' teacher in design business, under the worst conditions in the labor market, with everyone against, and with cumulative euphoria of reaching the big panorama of success, they give me the thanks of that job with what I reached my breaking point.

With the idea of employing me to start my own business after, I came to Merida. In Yucatan again. Looking for employment. Humidity 80 percent, average 38 degrees Celsius, the 'formal' shirt, tight fitting for sweat. Walk? My shoes about to break. A few coins on my pocket. My skin was burning. "You have to follow, always follow! New schools; other companies. What better way!" But ... The same story. I realized confabulations, cronyism, and too much regional discrimination. At the same time, lunges against my entrepreneurship, again and again. From potential business partners who were looking for me, and claimed to be my partners, not wanting to sign a contract. Then, how they want to do things right? They were lunges from one and another person, everybody were critical without knowing what the business I was working on was about; encroachments my chores without respecting my time, my space, or my stuff to work; or dislikes when I achieved a step forward, or because I have my life with understanding. I eluded everything that would minimize my work. Also they bothered with me when not hire me. If they saw I was living a new beginning, why they showed all the signs of not wanting to see someone stand up? This happened even those who least expects.

And this has a why. It is evident, because in the bottom they allow themselves to believe that if they cannot leave where they are, minus will make someone who has gone through a big bump and is rising again. And thus they are projecting that they are the ones do not accept life as it is, and therefore, they do not know the true path to success.

So at the end of 2013, sick of the situation, I set to work thoroughly on describe that unique energy of nature that creates reality. The force that is everywhere and is expressed in three different frequencies but you have to activate. Energy that I did not find awake in people, but I know with certainty that we all carry within and that is activated in the same way to be developed in business, that I once wanted to apply in a company.

Perhaps it takes me long to spread the way I looked business work. Now I know that was part of my maturing process in search of how to activate the triune force. However, from now on I know that this combined will get the best fruits. Because now that energy that I mean will be activated in you. For it is the force that makes it possible to rise from scratch and has already developed in business to achieve what we all seek; financial freedom. For the moment, I just want you to forge this as Tequila Sunrise for Business, because I know that:

Succeeding is to combine your intelligence and enthusiasm. If all you have left is just get up, take them and get what you love.

ARTIUX

Business background
Breaking the ice

Don't let the fear of losing be greater than the excitement of winning
ROBERT KIYOSAKI
American investor, businessman, self-help author, motivational speaker and
financial literacy activist

Large transnational companies have been characterized as highly successful organisms, especially with regard to joint dominance of the three key ingredients that make consumer appeal in the international market. Nonetheless, to stay connected to this system and immersed in the current globalization phenomenon and which it is almost impossible be isolated, are required to enter quickly and efficiently the strategies to ensure the true differential force that triggers win in business and apply them correctly as seen in commercial firms with high levels of development.

Part of this is shown by a study of Bruce, Cooper, & Vazquez (1999) applied to small businesses in the United Kingdom in which their results suggest that small businesses need to increase their interest in the design and incorporate it as an important process on their companies, including companies that took advantage of the design and they appreciated as a beneficial element for success of their projects. The study notes that one of the main causes of failure of design in this type of companies is the lack of interest and commitment that entrepreneurs show towards design.

Similarly, Iduarte & Zarza (2004) studied how the Micro, Small and Medium Enterprises (MSMEs) in the state of Estado de Mexico make use of professional design services, they consider that knows the methods of administering it and know how to apply on these segment of businesses, increase knowledge of designers about how is that micro, small and medium entrepreneurs manage and take advantage of design. They indicate that despite the fact that the design is considered as a very

1

important element, it is clear that there is a low design understanding and commitment by managers and that a high percentage of design projects is done by themselves or are in charge their friends and acquaintances.

The study suggests that entrepreneurs see design as an external process, cheaper, and for occasional acquisition, rather than perceiving it as a necessary and integrated business process in the company.

Is worth mentioning that although a large percentage of employers indicated that the contracted designers showed a passive attitude, misunderstanding the requirements and business conditions, constant delays in the process and lack of experience, refer that the effective use of design can contribute positively to the differentiation and functioning of the company. However, the authors claim that small businesses are often unaware of the business impact that can generate investment in design.

Likewise, in a study conducted by Guijosa & Frías (2006) to a sample of 253 consumers of different social classes residents of Mexico City and the Estado de Mexico, was sought if the tangible product attributes are important as part of the intent at the time making the purchase. Secondly identify whether additionally, consumers have in mind or consider at the time of purchase subjective aspects of symbolic type.

Regarding the first raised specific objective, evidence was found indicating that the design is conceived as a set of tangible attributes related to a sense of belonging and self-satisfaction and influences purchasing choices of an individual is found so that their preference lean toward for the "aesthetic looks" of a product but the need variable is in between because your choice is limited by the quality.

The results of the second objective of the study founded indicate that buying motives have to do with a line of reasoning value for money, based on subjective aspects; a symbolic added value of emotional affective nature, through stimuli, feelings and symbolism that design communicates.

Also, Google in December 2011 published online the "ZMOT e-book: Winning the Zero Moment of Truth," which showed the new mental model now proposed by the consumer.

In this paper, global CEO of Saatchi & Saatchi X, Dina Howell says, "We recently conducted a study to understand the emotional benefits that drive and influence shopping behavior. Those benefits, we found, include the satisfaction of deep needs for self-creation, mastery, security and connection. Shoppers today want to explore and think about how products can improve their lives. They do reconnaissance to gain the insights they need, and they're driven to bond with others and enrich relationships as they learn. They are motivated by a desire to take charge of their own identities and the well-being of their families and homes."

The study suggests that there is now another crucial moment of decision that happens before consumers get to the store. No matter what you sell, customers will be carried first impression of a product, and quite possibly will make the final decision on the Zero Moment of Truth (ZMOT): 24/7 global consumer interaction that allows companies win the day.

Selecting the best ice cubes

Ignorant of the XXI century are not those who cannot write or read, are those who cannot learn and unlearn and relearn
ALVIN TOFFLER
American writer and futurist Ph.D. in Literature

The above studies suggest on the one hand, that the benefits that design can bring their companies are unknown, on the other, that is managed with mismanagement by omitting the integration of design as an internal process of the company and finally, a higher and more accurate focus is required in the use of marketing to satisfy the aesthetic and emotional benefits consumers looking. Disciplines to be properly taken as advantage can ensure the proper execution of the project, adequate market acceptance and efficiency in the functioning of the company.

In sum, there has been a phenomenon in the critical moment of purchase decision, in which to focus efforts mentioned can lead to consumer participation endorsement, that it is vital now to win in business.

If we observe the business landscape, situating us within like generators and from outside as their end consumers, supported by indicators of previous studies, there may be enough evidence pointing to a lack of attention and knowledge:

First, among MSMEs towards the three disciplines, that act as the main pillars of business, that well developed jointly can define the aggrandizement of a company and generate better products that satisfy the changing demands of the market.

Then, the emergence of a new purchasing model based on the information sharing consumers about the best products, which largely determines a new moment in the process, where the buyers needs are satisfied, that will influence the success or failure of most brands in the world.

Adding the needed ice cubes

There is no challenge we cannot achieve by working together, with clear objectives and knowing the tools
CARLOS SLIM
Mexican businessman and philanthropist

Business with this recipe requiring the correct dose of ice, which contributes greatly with the required objective to comply in business, achieve success.

The ice here complements Tequila Sunrise for Business, than in this case it is necessary to stimulate you to get what you want to achieve, so that you have real bases and that observe how it is possible correctly project yourself to success with a business project, it is the testimony of 9 of the world's richest entrepreneurs.

This testimonies as success stories, shows and have sufficient elements to consider them as a reference, because each of these, fits perfectly with the development of the cocktail ingredients, that is, Tequila, Orange, and Grenadine, by which corresponds to the development of business in general, in the great diversity of their successful movements; as regards the work of each advice in particular, which together as a whole collaborate to build the Sunrise in a company. And I know that they, will express the best experience as part of the fantasy Tequila Sunrise, I have chosen for you. Ice whose name: Top 9 rules Tequila Sunrise for success, of world's billionaires. The testimonies of billionaires presented here, are part of the best ice cubes selected that make the glass resonate and showing the mettle of Tequila Sunrise for Business.

Echoing the right tumbler

If you don't build your dream, someone will hire you to help build their
DHIRUBHAI AMBANI
Indian Business Tycoon

Tequila Sunrise, is a brief record of how Works the commercial system of artificial reality under which we live. It is the entrance to the knowledge of the triune energy that sustains the natural system and that its creative force has developed by nature in the society but has been established the sense of corporation, commercialization and consumerism to not let see the true origin of this energy, constructing the name of commercial system that has fit very well in the world. However, being the only system that everyone recognizes in order to obtain sustenance and mainly the dominant business levels use to thrive and achieve success, it is urgent to know not only to survive but to be able to dominate in the Matrix and continue to contribute to the development of our society

To speak of the triune energy in business is because within the Matrix, in the system under which we live, this energy of course began to be expressed as a mental projection of its digital entity. Every time humanity has made progress and new ideas for the well-being and quality of life, by nature they are based on the triune energy that generates a condensation that is ordered, expanded and evidenced with the same intention with which it is created as the nature. However, in order to be manipulated by a few through history, to this mental projection to create was conferred the pose of a holographic generator of objects of desire and incorporated into business. It settled in the mentality of all like the only goal of illusions to follow, in order to obtain more and more capital goods and mass consumption. As the only way of obtaining welfare flaunting wealth. An idea difficult to eradicate.

Nevertheless, the ingredients of the triune energy seek harmony by random impulses of creation, to return to order, expansion and evidence, adapted in the best way to the situation.

So Tequila Sunrise for Business is the gap opened before your eyes that illuminates your vision so that you can lean on the system with the force of truth. It intends to change the paradigm of not being able to own a successful business. It aims to eradicate the implanted programming of obstacles and shortages with which you live, to establish the one of fluency and abundance through the businesses that you want to live.

The programming with which you will move the business and the base you are going to learn is scrupulous, even so what you will need of your greater concentration will be the way in which you can make it work with a business parallel to the system. I am referring to one who can generate abundance and at the same time positively impact your life and genuinely that of others within the same system. Something I'll tell you about later.

In summary. The combined force with which all things work, found cause to sprout within the Matrix. It took shape through the egregor that the system and society endowed it like commercial system. However the grandeur of life always knows how to return to its original state.

I have noticed it because I recognize the beauty in which life is expressed to create reality and after my search to decipher it I distinguished how it has developed in society because in my journey, in addition to love for what I do, I have felt the negative impact of the system on my life, but I did not let myself fall, I preferred to get up even if I started from scratch creating my own reality.

Placed the containers on the bar

I knew that if I failed I wouldn't regret that, but I knew the one thing I might regret is not trying
JEFF BEZOS
American founder & CEO

The projects do not walk alone, they need your intent and your desire to finally materialize.

By this I mean, if you really want to achieve success, you are leaving a possibility as a tendency to exist in reality, if you are very specific in how you want it and you work hard to get what you need, in a nutshell you are gathering the energy necessary for it to project in your reality, and therefore You are opening a vortex, which will accommodate the accumulation of energy that you have generated, ordering as you have arranged to detonate with the same force that you wanted to make it come true, a reality that is waiting for you.

Therefore choose well what you really want, what you will drive full force of your intention, that objective will be in who will download the best of you if you know give the right frequency to each ingredient to achieve business you expect. And if you do, that you really want will result of this, will accommodate to your request to harmonize with you.

Select well your collaborators, your representative segment, and your target market; to find your faithful consumer correctly. That is, choose well ice you need, they represent the same intention that want to take as a result.

Once you have ready on the bar the elements you need, both the tumbler receive the prepare, as the ice cubes will give vigor to this, then poured one by one the ingredients that you have developed in your business and gives its qualities to your firm, your brand, and your services or products. The pouring of the ingredients will take strength, flavor, and consistency upon contact with ice cubes that you chose and combine each and every one of them. It will endow its effects to your end consumer, based on what they want and at the times requires it.

Adjust the correct doses will be given you, until achieving a cocktail at his point. I truly hope that through Tequila Sunrise for Business you get the reality you want.

Serving the Tequila on business
Administration

Management is efficiency in climbing the ladder of success; leadership determines whether the ladder is leaning against the right wall
STEPHEN COVEY
American educator, author, businessman, and keynote speaker

As the first ingredient of Tequila Sunrise for Business, its function is to form the structure by which the conduct of your business will build. Its main task, is to provide the active substance shall grant character to the objectives of your company, in order to maintain its presence on business, and manage their effects to your audience.

According Chiavenato (2001) the word administration comes from the Latin *ad* (management, trend) and *minister* (subordination or obedience) meaning, fulfillment of a function under the command of another, namely, providing a service to another. However, the original meaning of this word has undergone a radical transformation.

The administration, as we know it today, is the historical outcome and integrated cumulative contribution of many pioneers philosophers, physicists, economists, statisticians and even entrepreneurs that over time were developing and disseminating works and theories in their field activities. It is therefore not surprising that widely use certain modern management concepts and principles discovered in the mathematical sciences, as statistics; the human sciences such as psychology, sociology, education or biology; in the physical sciences like physics or chemistry; as well as law and engineering among others.

On the way emerged important management theories that have their main approaches and each one favors a variable that emphasizes the point of view from which it develops. Although by itself the content of management study varies widely by theory or school considered, somehow all administrative theories are applicable to current situations to be used in each context, therefore management has become one of the most significant human activity areas.

Despite all the progress made by human knowledge, the called management science flourished just in the early twentieth century, and it was a historical event of significance.

The administration is an important activity in a pluralistic society based on cooperation activities that people develop in organizations. From the moment in which organizations reached a certain size and complexity, administration began to present difficulties and challenges hitherto ignored by managers, who needed new administrative developments.

This process is ongoing and requires a set of people in different hierarchical levels that deal with different issues, therefore management has become one of the most important areas of human activity. By living in a civilization where the cooperative effort of the people is the fundamental base of society, the administration is essential to the existence, survival and success of organizations.

Hence arose the growing need to develop a theory of management that allowed offer managers of organizations suitable models and strategies to solve their business problems.

In this regard it is important to know some definitions of management to enrich our landscape and understand the general meaning of discipline:

Taylor, mentioned in Chiavenato (2001) argues that the administration has emphasis on the tasks performed within a company when to focus attention on improving the effectiveness of the company is first required to meet the increased efficiency at the operational level.

To Fayol (as cited in Chiavenato 2001), the administration is an applied social science that studies the organizations responsible for planning, organizing, directing, coordinating and controlling the resources of an organization (human, financial, material, technological, intellectual, and so on) in order to obtain the maximum possible economic or social benefit, according to its objectives, in which the company start of a synthetic, global and universal approach that begins with its anatomical and structural conception as an organization. For him, administration is a whole of which the organization is one of the parts, and only refers to the establishment of the structure and form, so it is static and limited. La organización formal se basa en la división del trabajo racional, está planeada en el papel, explicada, descrita con reglas, procedimientos y cargos. The informal organization appears spontaneously among friends and groups of antagonism without appearing on a chart, or any other formal document.

According to Kaplan (2014) the administration is an intercultural and social management based on an interdisciplinary approach.

García Padilla (2014) said that, since modern management of an organization is centered on strategy and focused on customer needs, it is possible to conceive of administration, such as management developed human talent to facilitate the work of a group workers within an organization. In order to meet overall goals, both institutional and personal, regularly goes hand in hand with the application of techniques and principles of the administrative process, where the leading role is optimal and efficient development, creating certainty in the conduct of the people and the application of different resources.

Basic concept: The management process is the result of the basic activity of collaboration towards a common goal, which is manifested by the concepts of organization and strategy aimed at business.

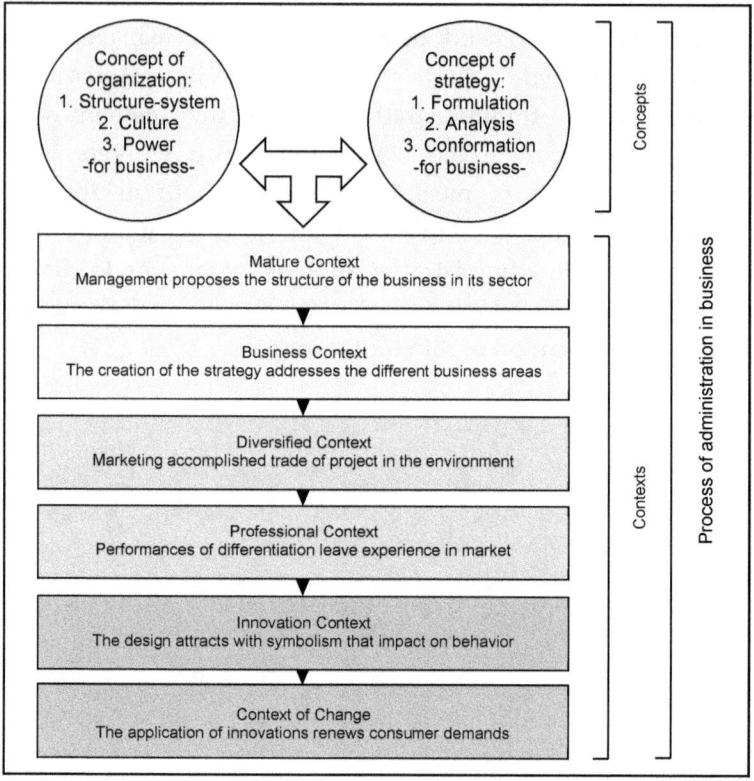

The administration process in business. Adapted from: Mintzberg, Henry; J. Brian; J. Voyer. *El proceso estratégico. Conceptos, contextos y casos.* [The strategic process. Concepts, contexts and cases]. Mexico: Prentice Hall Hispano-American, 1997. 641 pp. intro.

Administration and business

An organization without human commitment is like a person without a soul
HENRY MINTZBERG
Internationally recognized Canadian academic and author on business

According to Chiavenato (2001) The General Administrative Theory (GAT) is the field of knowledge that deals with the study of administration in general and of all organizations. The chronology of the main events of the origins of the administration towards its subject matter has evolved since the beginning of civilization:

- 4000 B.C. The Egyptians recognized the need to plan, organize and control.
- 2600 B.C. Decentralize the organization.
- 2000 B.C. Recognize the written orders and consulting.
- 1800 B.C. Hammurabi uses the written control sets the minimum wage and acknowledges that responsibility cannot be transferred.
- 1491 B.C. The Hebrew achieves organizational concepts, scale and exception.
- 600 B.C. Nebuchadnezzar controls production and wage incentives.
- 500 B.C. Mencius in China recognizes the need for standard systems.
- 400 B.C. Cyrus in Persia and Socrates in Greece forth the universality of management and Plato the principle of specialization.
- 175 B.C. Cato in Rome uses the description of functions.
- 284. Diocletian delegates authority.
- 1436. Arsenal of Venice makes cost accounting, checks and balances to control inventory numbers, assembly line and staff management.
- 1525. Machiavelli begins consensus, cohesion and leadership.
- 1767. Sir James Stuart creates the source of authority, differentiation of hierarchies based on the advantages of specialization.
- 1776. Adam Smith in England begins specialization of workers and the concept of control with the use of the steam engine and its application to production during the Industrial Revolution.

• 1799. Eli Whitney in the United States employs quality control and recognizes the administrative amplitude.

• 1800. James Watt and Matthew Boulton in England standardized production, working methods, times, specifications, gives benefits and uses the audit.

• 1810. Robert Owen applied practices and training to employees and gives house plans.

• 1832. Charles Babbage emphasizes specialization, division of labor, time, motion and color effects on the efficiency of the labor applied in uniform and announcements.

• 1856. Daniel C. McCallum in the United States uses the chart to show the organizational structure.

• 1886. Henry Metcalfe employed the administration as art and science.

• Since 1900, begins The General Administrative Theory with industrial pioneers and entrepreneurs from big companies like General Electric, Singer, Rockefeller, Westinghouse, Ford, and so on. And it is Frederick W. Taylor who made possible by activating the evolution of what we now know as business management:

• In 1903 with scientific management using cooperation needs between workers and management, salary increases, exception principle applied to the production floor, study methods, time study, and emphasis on research, planning and control.

• It was followed in 1909 the theory of bureaucracy: With the emphasis on peaceful behavior of the internal elements of the company.

• After 1916 the classical theory by Henry Fayol: Emphasized in managing the main direction and subordination.

• In 1932 the theory of human relations: In an effort to decide all people in the organization.

• In 1947 structuralist theory: Concentrated in the intra-organizational analysis and business departments.

• In 1951 the systems theory: Giving full importance to the environment surrounding the company towards a socio-technical approach.

• In 1954 neoclassical theory: Highlighting the general principles of management and administrator functions.

- In 1957 behavioral theory: Emphasizing the styles of management and integration of individual decisions.
- In 1962 the theory of organizational development: Committed to organizational change planned for the growth of the company.
- By 1972 the situational theory focused on changes affecting the company with an environmental imperative and use of technology.
- And then the contingency theory: With the emphasis on how best to adapt to external changes with the use of technology.

In outlining the gradual steps of administration, the effect of the various theories with their contributions and valid points for any organization or company is shown. Although each theory arose as a response to business problems of his time, all administrative theories are applicable to current situations in business.

In that sense, Wikipedia.org (2015) says that a business is to create or constitute an entity with a system, method or manner in order to get money for production activities (as does a factory), marketing (as does a store or a distributor) or services (as does an establishment or a workshop), that benefit others.

To start a business you need to develop a business model, this is understood as the type of activity to do with strategy, or planting of the factors or elements that make up the business. So the commercial or social activity that has been thought and that is to be developed is the core business. And formed a tool that allows us to organize and planning activities that must be performed to achieve the goals of our company cooperatively.

A well-run business must have a store displaying their products or services, to invite do different payment transactions. It consists of professionally perform the activities from production and beyond sales, personnel distributed at different hierarchical levels clearly defined responsibilities.

Basic concept: The active and productive life of companies only guarantees for those them to reach a sound understanding of its strategic responsibilities, disciplines that underpin and maturity of its business basic model. (Adapted from Colmenares, 1992, Intro.)

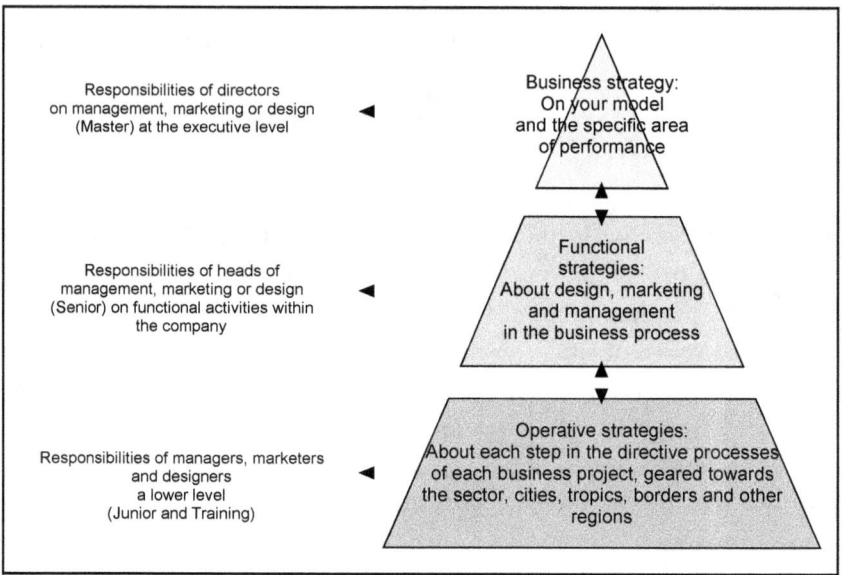

The Pyramid of the creation of the strategy in a company of single business. Adapted from: Thompson, Arthur; Strickland, A. J. *Strategic management. Concepts and cases.* USA: Mc Graw Hill, 2004. 398 pp. p. 53.

The purpose of administration

Whenever you see a successful business, someone once made a courageous decision
PETER DRUKER
Austrian-born, American management consultant, educator, and author

To Chiavenato (2001) the world today is a society composite of organizations oriented to production of goods or "products" and the provision of specialized activities or "services," which are planned, coordinated, directed and controlled in organizations, which are constituted by individuals and non-human resources. The lives of people dependent organizations and the latter depend on the work of the former. Some organizations are called corporations, whether or not for profit.

In any form of human endeavor, the efficiency with which people work together to achieve common goals depends primarily on the ability of those who exercise administrative functions, this function is performed in each discipline within an organization.

Each company should be considered from the point of view of the effectiveness and efficiency simultaneously.

1. Effectiveness is a measure of achievement of results.
2. Efficiency is a measure of resource utilization in the process.

Although the recent administrative theory has shifted the focus of "a better way," endeavor to achieve the best project without determining the correct strategy, towards the approach of "everything depends on," or achieving a good strategy and adapt to the context depending on the market movements; every organization needs to be managed in an appropriate way to achieve their goals more efficiently and effectively. The ideal would be an efficient and effective company, which constitute excellence.

Nowadays the administration, studies companies and other types of organizations, from the point of view of interaction and interdependence among six main variables:

1. People: the skills of business professionals.
2. Environment: developing business industry chosen.
3. Tasks: the administrative process in every area of business.

4. Structure: the distribution of responsibilities within the company.

5. Technology: the tools and the most appropriate means.

6. Competitiveness: Tactical differentiator, contact and visual.

Each which is specific object of study by the administrative theory and are essential components in the study of business administration.

The behavior of these components is systemic and complex because each influences and is influenced by other components. The changes that take place in one cause changes greater or lesser degree in others. Overall behavior is different from the sum of the behavior of each component considered separately. The new variable, competitiveness, complements each and every one of the above variables; it incorporates the necessary push to mobilize that complex whole in the pursuit of excellence, thus avoiding the compliance.

Due to the increasing importance of management and new and complex challenges it faces, the balance is variously inclined to certain individual aspects of the enormous context of variables involved in the structure and behavior of organizations.

In the coming decades, major management challenges will:

1. Growth of organizations: Successful organizations tend to the growth and expansion of its activities, either in terms of size and resources, expand their markets or the size of their operations.

2. Fierce competition: As more markets and business, so do the risks in business. The product or service that proves to be superior or better will be the one with higher demand.

3. Sophistication of technology: With the progress of communications, computer, and transport, organizations and companies have internationalized their operations and activities.

4. High inflation rates: The costs of energy, raw materials, labor force and money are continually rising. Inflation requires increasingly greater efficiency in business so they can get better results with the available resources and reducing operating costs.

5. Economic globalization and internationalization of business: Export activity and the creation of new subsidiaries in foreign territories are a recent phenomenon, which will influence the future organization and management. Competition becomes worldwide due to global trade.

6.   Greater role of organizations: As they grow, organizations become more competitive, technologically sophisticated, and more international and, with this, increase its environmental impact.

The major management challenges related to adapt and integrate the six variables mentioned.

In this regard, Chiavenato notes that the adequacy and integration among these six variables are the main management challenges. And also mentions that as the administration is facing new situations that arise over time and space, administrative doctrines and theories need to adapt their approaches or modify them to remain useful and applicable. This explains, in part, the gradual steps from the General Theory of Administration, over time, and the breadth and complexity gradual.

The basic task of management is to carry out activities in an orderly manner with the participation of all people immersed in that process, interpret the objectives proposed by an organization and transform them into teamwork through planning, organizing, the direction and control of all activities in their areas and levels, in order to achieve those objectives in the most appropriate manner to the situation.

So, that Mintzberg, Brian, & Voyer (1997) say that the structure of the overall strategy must reflect the situation of the organization:

1.   Their age.
2.   Size or number of members.
3.   The type of production system or tasks.
4.   The degree of complexity and dynamism of technology and its environment.

They mention that, as some organizations have cultures underdeveloped or cultures that are not distinctive at all and these organizations with weak cultures can be considered unsuccessful in stylistic terms.

And moreover, as companies with strong cultures, by coincidence or by design, can be considered rich in stylistic terms, whose members identify with the organization and committed to values and beliefs that are inspirational, where these values contribute to the stability of the organization and are an instrument used to the new members to understand the events and activities that occur in there.

Organizational culture is important to understand a number of intangible elements that are shared by members of an organization; their values, beliefs that guide their actions, innuendoes, and even how to think.

Therefore we must skillfully address the two levels on which occurs normally organizational culture:

The observable level such as clothing people behavior and material environment.

As the deep level that represents the true culture and rituals, ceremonies, stories, symbols and language.

As the basics of culture and organizational strategy that will help fulfill the purpose of the administration.

Basic concept: All variables of an organization are directed to productive teamwork, they maintain interdependence in all senses for proper interaction between their activities.

Basic variables of management within an organization. Adapted from: Chiavenato, Idalberto. *Introducción a la teoría general de la administración*. [Introduction to general management theory]. Mexico: McGraw-Hill, 2001. 1056 pp. p. 14.

The strategic direction of management

Formal education will make you a living. Self-education will make you a fortune
JIM ROHN
Important American business philosopher

Chiavenato (2001) indicates that administration arises from the conception that every business can be divided into six groups called the basic management functions:

1.   Technical Functions: related to the production of goods and services of the company.

2.   Commercial Functions: related to the purchase, sale and exchange.

3.   Financial Functions: related to the search and management of capital.

4.   Safety Features: relating to the protection and preservation of goods and people.

5.   Accounting Functions: related to inventories, records, balances, costs and statistics.

6.   Administrative Functions: related to the integration of the other five functions of management. Administrative functions coordinate and synchronize the other functions of the company and are always above them.

These latter functions, administrative, thus defining the act of managing according Fayol (in Chiavenato 2001) and containing the universal functions of management who are the called administrative process are present in any activity manager at any level or area of activity of the company:

1.   Planning: visualize the future and chart a program of action.

2.   Organizing: building the physical and social structures of the company.

3.   Directing: guiding and orienting staff.

4.   Coordinating: link, unite and harmonize all acts and collective efforts.

5.   Controlling: check that everything happens according to established rules and orders given.

Any member of a company performs these functions by participating in these guidelines from any level.

Hil & Jones (2005) explain that to correctly carry these administrative functions throughout the organization should focus attention on the strategic process, it analyzes all the functions of a company defines its action through appropriate strategies and headed inside and outside the company in order to get the best results.

In this manner, administration introduces the concept of situational analysis refers to analyzing the internal and external environment in which the analysis of the position of the company is made. This analysis involves a combination of strengths, weaknesses, threats and opportunities facing a business.

The strategic management process consists of five components:

1.   The selection of the mission and major corporate goals.

2.   The analysis of the external differentiation environment of the organization to identify *Opportunities and Threats*.

3.   Analysis of the internal operating environment of the organization, which highlights its *Strengths and Weaknesses*.

4.   The selection of strategies based on the *strengths* of the organization and corrects their *weaknesses* in order to take advantage of external *opportunities* and to counter external *threats*.

5.   The implementation of the strategy. The company expects the implementation of its resources by way of achieving your goals and accomplish adapt as best as possible to their environment.

Analyze the environments is called strategy formulation. The implementation of strategies involves the settings on organizational structures and control systems to put into action the strategy. This analysis is known as (SWOT) *Strengths, Weaknesses, Opportunities and Threats*.

Under this scenario as Thompson & Strickland (1998) we see that the SWOT analysis forms a matrix that is transcendental for organizations.

In its first phase are those that form part of the internal environment and indicate the variables on which the company can take action.

1.   The strengths; that are positive, including: • Fundamental capabilities in key areas • Adequate financial resources • Good image buyers • A recognized leader in the market • Strategies well designed functional areas • Access to economies of scale • Isolated (at least to some degree) of strong competitive pressures • Technology ownership • Cost

advantages • Best advertising campaigns • Skills for product innovation • Management able • Advantageous position in the experience curve • Best manufacturing capacity • Superior technological skills.

2.   The weaknesses; they are negative, such as: • No clear strategic direction • Obsolete facilities • Lower profitability average • Lack of opportunity and talent management • Poor monitoring in implementing the strategy • Abundance of internal operational problems • Delay in research and development • Line products too limited • Weak market image • Weak distribution network • Skills marketing below • Inability to finance the necessary changes in strategy • Higher general unit costs in relation to key competitors.

In its second phase are those forming part of the external environment and are factors which cannot be modified by the will of the company.

3.   The threats; they are negative, as: • Entry of foreign competitors with lower costs • Increased sales and substitute products • Slower growth in the market • Adverse changes in exchange rates and trade policies of foreign governments • Costly regulatory requirements • Vulnerability recession and business cycle • Increased bargaining power of customers or suppliers • Change in the needs and tastes of buyers • Adverse demographic changes.

4.   And the opportunities; that are positive, such as: • Addressing additional customer groups • Entering new markets or segments • Expand the product line to satisfy a wider range of customer needs • Diversifying into related products • Vertical integration (forward or backward) • Removing trade barriers in foreign markets attractive • Complacency among the rival companies • Fastest growth in the market.

The administrator must identify the factors on which work hard, first to remove those within the category of risky and secondly to protect and enrich those who favor him.

Basic Concept: The strategic management process raises the mission statement of the company tends to focus on their business perspective (who we are and what we do) generally describes the capabilities of the company, its strategic approach and the current appearance their businesses.

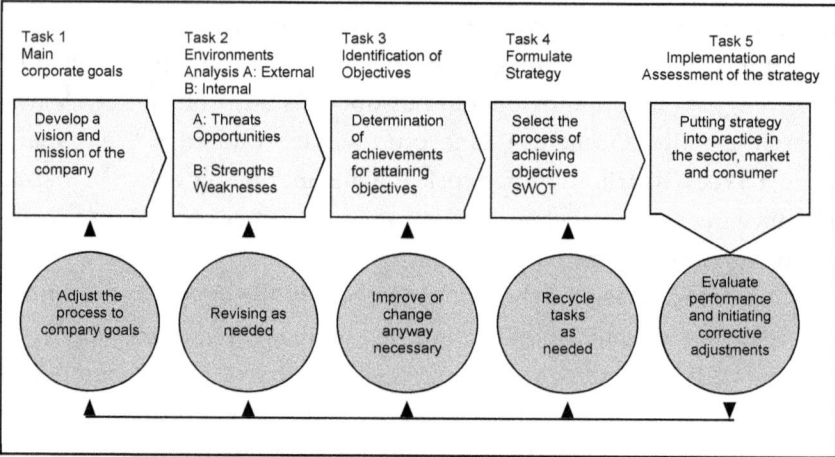

The five tasks of strategic management. Adapted from: Thompson, Arthur; Strickland, A. J. *Strategic management. Concepts and cases.* USA: Mc Graw Hill, 2004. 398pp. p. 7. And: Hill, Charles W. L.; Jones, Gareth R. *Administración estratégica. Un enfoque integrado.* [Strategic management. An integrated approach]. Mexico: McGraw-Hill Interamericana, 2005. 915 pp. p. 10.

The business plan

Thinking out a plan and ensuring its success is one of the keenest satisfaction for
an intelligent man to experience
HENRY FAYOL
French engineer and director of mines, theoretical of business administration

When starting your business project can easily happen to forget the business plan, considering that to have found a need in the market and provide a product or service, necessarily will succeed. However, if there is no strong planning, it is certainly not sustain growth.

Make a business plan raises the possibility succeed and grow. Develop a strategy means knowing the map indicating where you will take your project and you must start from a SWOT analysis already mentioned to capture it in a document called a business plan.

According to *Comisión Nacional para la Protección y Defensa de los Usuarios de Servicios Financieros (Condusef)* [National Commission for the Protection and Defense of Users of Financial Services] (2013) business plan is a guidance document for the employer whereby, processed, define and evaluate aspects that make up the idea or project business. This document is for the entrepreneur who seeks to realize his idea for the business when you want to define your project and for investors seeking to convince always new candidates to participate as partners in business.

Develop a business plan in a document allows the observation of likely future scenarios and variables, in order to facilitate a comprehensive analysis when seating the final position chosen. Allows imagine ideas, solutions and results, to be clear how to turn them into reality. It's also a map that can be presented to other parties involved in the project as investors, partners, banks, suppliers and customers.

The advantages of a business plan are varied, marks the moment in the life of the company and the type or business model to be planned. Ensures a business has operational and financial sense, prior to commissioning. Seek the most efficient way of carrying out a project. Create a panorama that identifies needs, avoid obstacles and allocate resources previously to the fact, taking leads to savings in time, money and effort. Evaluate the performance having an ongoing business. Help make improvements to business processes. It is a guide to correct the path and cause changes to the business.

Develop a business plan allows to establish a significant and necessary distance between changes unfounded (occurrences) and business decisions foundation (planning) taken based on the information and analysis.

The process to be followed to make a business plan varies according to each company, but in general it is advisable to consider the following points:

Mature or specify the business idea to perform. Organize all the information available to capture aspects that affect business operations, review what information is missing and get it. Assess if you can do it yourself, or require the participation of other individuals or teams and external professionals, area managers, employees, and so on.

For Berry (2014) all movement of the company is important to have a plan. So to know where you're going, you need to know where you come from and what path you traveled. Here are some general elements of a successful business plan.

1.   Description of Business. You must define various aspects of your offer as the context of your industry, service address, and the purpose of your contribution, your business goals and general objectives in the short, medium and long term. This section is the backbone of your business plan and prepares the stage for the rest of the information.

2.   Products and services. All have a product or service that is aimed at a target audience. You must be able to describe what you sell and identify what makes your product unique.

3.   Sales and marketing. This section opens the window industry, market conditions, general costs and gives you the opportunity to distinguish yourself from the competition. Describe how you see your merchandise and branding to be recognized at scales from the personal to the global.

4.   Operations. The purpose of this aspect is to help highlight the administrative side of your business, including how you move, the location of your office, equipment management, public relations, network providers, and so on.

5.   Human talent. One that is, if you have consultants, partners, directors or people to help in your business, this is where you understand

their involvement and ability to contribute to your success. If there is a hierarchy of positions within your company and the relevance of each relationship.

6.   Development. The part where you can imagine the visionary management. Not everything in this section is based on the facts as the information itself you bring in the other sections. Here you project into the future and think big. The development is an important part of the business to continue differentiating you, you should be sure to complete these visions to land them into goals.

7.   Financial Summary. Where composing a history of your investments, financial dealings and how you managed to get the position you have now. With some flexibility, you'll understand how to operate your business; you'll see your financial statement, including how the numbers are balanced at the end of each month, the health of your business and cash flow.

8.   Executive Summary. It is a composition of one or two pages of your business plan. It is best done when you finished all the details of the plan.

According Myownbusiness.org (2013) the main value of the business plan is to create the project in writing that evaluates all aspects of the viability of the business venture describing and analyzing business expectations. The preparation and maintenance of a business plan is important for any industry regardless of size or money. But does not guarantee success. If not properly value their potential, then the business plan could become a guide to failure. If a proper assessment of the economic changes of business is maintained, the plan will not only be a useful guide but also a financial tool for success.

This is an essential step you should take as a prudent businessman, regardless of the size of your business.

Basic Concept: The business plan format in 13 steps focuses on the essential actions that yield a maximum investment.

1.	DESCRIPTION OF BUSINESS:
2.	NICHE MARKETS:
3.	TERRITORIES OR GEOGRAPHICAL COVERAGE OF BUSINESS:
4.	DESIRED POSITIONING:
5.	BUSINESS UNIQUE PROPOSAL:
6.	BASIC INVESTMENT TO DEVELOP THE BUSINESS:
Identify the amount to invest to start the business, as well as the origin or source and the conditions of financial resources (contributions, loan, society, and so on).	
7.	FINANCIAL GOALS:
In 3 months; in 6 months; 12 months; 24 months; 36 months.	
8.	TYPE AND NUMBER OF UNITS SOLD:
Products; Services; Packages; (Include quantity to sell and date must achieve the target) Name; Product Type; Existing develop; Estimated selling units Quantity; Estimated Sales Price; Scheduled date for achieving the goal sales.	
9.	PRICES:
10.	MEANS OF MARKETING FOR THESE NICHES:
11.	GOALS OF MARKETING: (development of marketing tools and applications to achieve the above sales).
Identifying the stages of development and compliance required to have a means of marketing complete and ready for use in business.	
Medium; Components; Description; Start; End; Expected product.	
12.	GOALS FOR DEVELOPMENT OF NEW PRODUCTS; Services; Packages; Product Type; Name; Start; End; (repeated for each different product).
13.	PROMOTIONAL MATERIALS:

Format of basic business plan. Adapted from: *Nacional Financiera (Nafin)* [National Financer] (2009). *13 pasos para hacer tu plan de negocios. Guía del participante*. [13 steps to make your business plan. Participant guide]. 32 pp.
capacitación@nafin.gob.mx, www.nafin.gob.mx/portalnf/get?file=/pdf/otros/TRECE-PASOS.pdf

Here, one of the three elements that causes ice force, is the vigor. Which should be impregnated in the tequila to maintain the good development of the cocktail. I mean to vigor, such as the business plan.

TEQUILA SUNRISE FOR BUSINESS

Basic Concept: The business plan is the tool that projects all activities of an organization regardless of size. Must be done from entrepreneurship and renewed according to changes in the lifetime of the company.

I.	ASPECTS OF MARKET AND MARKETING

1. Business detail. 2. Description of the product. 3. Description of services. 4. Specific objectives. 5. General objectives. 6. Philosophy. 7. Securities. 8. Mission. 9. Vision. 10. Market opportunities that give rise to the project. 11. Motivation. 12. Profile whom it is directed. 13. Market research. 14. Economic density product. 15. Feasibility of business development. 16. Main clients. 17. Major competitors. 18. Major suppliers. 19. Timing of product on the market. 20. Geographical distribution. 21. Supply and demand. 22. Rates and prices. 23. Plus product. 24. Policies and sales strategies.

II.	TECHNICAL ASPECTS

1. Condition and operation of the project. 2. Location. 3. Reason for the location. 4. General Resources. 5. Permissions. 6. Appropriate size of the facility. 7. Architectural plan. 8. Effects of energy use. 9. Estimated ecological impact. 10. Wastewater discharge. 11. Organic waste. 12. Inorganic waste. 13. The availability and quality of raw materials. 14. Production capacity. 15. Product Requirements. 16. Quality Control. 17. Scope of strategic point. 18. Scope of point of differentiation. 19. Scope of point innovation. 20. Development of global communication. 21. Consistency of corporate identity and brand.

III.	ADMINISTRATIVE ASPECTS

1. Timing of activities: general description processes. 2. Schedule of activities: Duration of individual projects. 3. Strategic Conduct. 4. Management skills. 5. Professionalism of human talent. 6. Description of skilled labor. 7. Number of adequate staff. 8. Age of the organization. 9. Internal rules. 10. General Flowchart: Flow of the organizational structure. 11. Letter distribution of activities: Who does what and how much you earn. 12. Sustainability of the project: In what success is based. 13. Benefits. 14. Concerns. 15. State of the socio-economic environment in which the project is developed.

IV.	ECONOMIC-FINANCIAL ASPECTS

1. Budgets. 2. Investment. 3. Working capital. 4. Analysis WWISS: How I have to Work, Winning, and Investing, Saving, and Spending. 5. Statement. 6. Inflation. 7. Exchange. 8. Taxation. 9. Bank interest rate. 10. Convenience. 11. Recovery of invested capital. 12. Risk project. 13. Yields.

V.	SOCIAL ASPECTS

Benefit of project to society. 2. Direct effects. 3. Indirect Effects. 4. Magnitude of effects. 5. Sustainability of the project.

Format of business plan. Adapted from: *Nacional Financiera (Nafin)* [National Financer] (2002). capacitación@nafin.gob.mx

Strategy

A strategy delineates a territory in which a company seeks to be unique
MICHAEL PORTER
Professor at the Harvard Business School and global authority on strategy

Mintzberg et al., (1997) notes that the term strategy comes from the Greek *"strategos"* which means *"general."* In turn comes from roots meaning *"army"* and *"lead." Stratego* the Greek verb meaning "to plan the destruction of the enemy by reason of efficient use of resources."

The concept of strategy in a military and political context is well known for hundreds of years. In the case of modern competitive business with inclination to project strategies companies try to outperform their rivals.

To understand the role of business strategy, Mintzberg, discusses two approaches to the concept of strategy as distinguished as "School of design" and "School planning," mentions that the definitions of strategy that have been made since then are only changes in definitions of their authors Andrews and Ansoff respectively. And all these definitions have four things in common, so you might consider a uniform landscape of strategy in business.

The strategy from the point of view of the administration provides the next horizon:

1.   The environment: Internal and external, or own and outside company conditions to which you must respond. To implement business strategy in each process.

2.   The mission: A definition of the reason for existence of the company. To establish the true purpose of the company.

3.   The analysis of the situation: The processes to be performed to determine how pro their situation in the environments is. Be strengths or weaknesses (in the internal environment) or threats or opportunities (in the external environment).

4.   The application of resources: Towards the environment in which it competes. Resulting in the achievement of its objectives.

Therefore, the selection of a strategy should establish a position in the means in which it is developed and being this, a sector in business, market overview then arises.

So to Kotler & Armstrong (2003) establishing marketing strategy consists of the following components:

1.   Responding to the primary requirements of the company and observe the demands wake up in the market.

2.   Identify the competitive advantages on which to cement a position.

3.   Select the right and choose an overall business strategy for positioning.

4.   Communicate effectively and present the position chosen to market specifically to your target audience.

In this case each company should differentiate its offering by creating a unique package of competitive advantages.

From this perspective, when approached the target audience is that you can appreciate closely the strategy that requires the product, so it is possible to see the design.

The design strategy for (Zimmermann, 1998) and strategic process according to (idologie, 2012) consists of the following items:

1.   Analysis of the end or design / *LEVEL* design project. New product or service; *Renewal* of design; *Continuity* for line extension. By understanding, observation and definition of the type of project: Consulting, research and benchmarks for the first mental projection. *(R-C)*

2.   Analysis creative of design project / Current *ENVIRONMENT* image. Positioning: Current and central *Promise*, product *Perception*, raison d'être of the brand to the consumer; consumer: profile, SEL; category: competition and trends. Analyze what customers have in mind about the brand. For them their perception is reality. This perception must be sought directly in the market and not try to ask the staff or think like customers. *(P-P)*

3.   Analysis of means / Select product *STRATEGY*. Product vs. competition: Shared *Values*, points of contact of the category and *Qualities* shared within the category; functional and emotional attributes, performance differentiator own and inherited values; disadvantages vs. competition, weaknesses of the product and how to minimize. *(V-Q)*

4.   Strategy Action / *IMPLEMENTATION* design and objectives action. Desired positioning: How you want to be identified by the market, which will differ in order to achieve what you want, what quality will communicate; to the consumer: Retain current, adding new, changing

ARTIUX

consumer, profile and SEL of the new consumer; vs. competition, what should be the new *Personality* and tone of *Communication*, branding opportunities that the client detects, social or visual restrictions. Research and opinion. Viable strategy positioning: Premise: cannot be many things at the same time. Image strategy: Generate brand value and emotional bond. *(P-C)*

Strategic process that analyzes both the attributes won: Level and the Environment; as proposed attributes: Strategy and Implementation. So I call (LESI) of the design project in its sphere of action.

Johnson, Whittington, & Scholes (cited by Free-management-ebooks.com, 2013) believe that "the strategy is the direction and scope of an organization over the long term, which achieves an advantage in an environmental change through its configuration of resources and expertise."

In general, Levy (1981) assures that the success of a company is the compatibility between environment and strategy. In this sense the strategic behavior entails adopting an appropriate strategic plan that includes goals, objectives and specific strategies:

1. The long-term plan: Estimated exceeding five years.
2. The medium-term plan: For periods between two and four years.
3. The short-term plan: For periods of one to two years.

Although each organization will have differences in requirements can be formulated three basic criteria for determining the planning horizon:

1. The accuracy of possible prediction of the chosen strategy.
2. The nature of the products on the market.
3. The commitment of the business model to future.

In this regard, Mintzberg (mentioned Hil & Jones, 2005) complements the administration intervenes when appropriate, discarding the bad strategies, whether these emerging (reactive adapted) or attempted (largely planned), but cultivating those potentially good.

However, Mintzberg et al., (1997) assert that "To make such decisions business managers must be able to judge the value of emerging strategies. Must be able to think strategically."

In general terms and for the build in your business, a strategy is a systematic series of actions planned in time, that are performed to accomplish a specific mission, which suits so well to benefit a company achieves differentiate uniquely.

Glimpsing the basic structure on which strategic thinking sits: competition.

Basic Concept: business administration must distinguish all kinds of strategies that are in part planned and reactive part, from its emergence and consider all your valuable components to achieve a better response to its purposes.

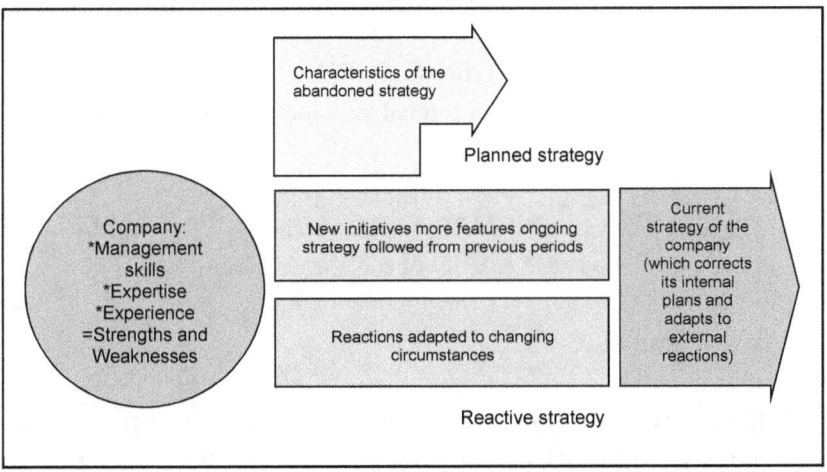

The strategy of a company. Adapted from: Thompson, Arthur; Strickland, A. J. *Strategic management. Concepts and cases.* USA: Mc Graw Hill, 2004. 398 pp. p. 12.

These 6 behaviors of the administration correspond to Tequila. Use them to project the character of your company and build a structure with a winning presence in the intellect of the people.
Make them think what they observe of your company

The ice on background | PART 1
Pervading Tequila

I am looking for a lot of men who have an infinite capacity to not know what can't be done
HENRY FORD
American industrial, founding and father of the modern production lines

RICHARD BRANSON
Founder & CEO of the Virgin Group

Take responsibility.

"I think I learned early on that, if you can run one company, you can really run any companies, I mean companies are all about finding the right people and inspiring those people, you know, and drawing out the best in people. And I just love learning, and I'm incredibly inquisitive, and I love taking on the status quo, and trying to turn it upside down. So I've seen life as one long learning process. And if I see, you know, if I fly on somebody else's airline and find the experiences is not a pleasant one, which it wasn't in 21 years ago, then I think, well, you know, maybe I can create the kind of airline that I'd like to fly on. And so, I got one second-hand 747 from Boeing and gave it a go [...] I think there's a very thin dividing line between success and failure. And I think if you start a business without financial backing, you're likely to go the wrong side of that dividing line. We were being attacked by British Airways. They were trying to put our airline out of business, and they launched what's become known as the 'dirty tricks campaign,' and I realized that, you know, the whole empire was likely to come crashing down, unless I chipped in a chip. And in order to protect the jobs of the people who worked for the airline, and protect the jobs of the the people who worked for the record company, I had to sell, you know, the family jewelry to protect the airline

[...] it was sad at the time, but we move on [...] I like to think it stands for quality, if somebody comes across a Virgin Company [...] We have a lot of fun, and I think the people who work for it, enjoy it. As I say, we go in, and shake up other industries, and I think, we do it differently, and I think, that industries are not quite the same as a result of Virgin attacking the market [...] I mean, I think, with the ballooning and boating expeditions we've done in the past, well, I got pulled out of the sea, I think, six times by helicopters, so and each time, I didn't expect to come home to tell the tale. So, in those moments, you certainly wonder, what you're doing up there? [...] I think the balloon adventures were, each one was, actually, I think, we came close. And I mean first of all, nobody had actually crossed the Atlantic in a hot air balloon before [...] The PR experts said that, as an airline owner, the last thing you should be doing is heading off in balloons and boats, and crashing into the seas. In fact, I think our airline took a full page ad at the time saying, 'common Richard, there are better ways of crossing the Atlantic' [...] I was dyslexic. I had no understanding of schoolwork whatsoever. I certainly would have failed IQ tests. And it was one of the reasons I left the school when I was 15 years old. And if I'm not interested in something, just I don't grasp it. As somebody is dyslexic, you also have some quite bizarre situations, sorted for instance, and I've had two, but you know, I have been running the largest group of private companies in Europe, but haven't been able to know the difference between net and gross. And so, the board meetings have been faster fascinating [...] I don't actually think that the stereotype of a business person, treading all over people to get to the top, and generally speaking works. I think if you treat people well, people will come back, and come back for more. And I think all you have in life is your reputation, and it's a very small world. And I actually think that the best way of becoming a successful business leader, is dealing with people fairly and well. And I like to think that's how we run Virgin [...] Capitalism has been proven to be a system that works, you know, the alternative, communism, he not does work. But the problem with capitalism is, extreme wealth ends up in the hands a few people, and therefore, extreme responsibility, I think, goes with that wealth. And I think it is important that the individuals, who are in that fortune position, do not end up competing for bigger and bigger boats, and bigger and bigger cars, but use that money, to either, create new jobs or to tackle issues around the world [...] I think that everybody, people do things for the whole variety of different reasons and I think that, you know, when I'm on my deathbed, I will want to feel that I've made a difference to other people's lives, and that, may be a selfish thing to think, but it's the way I've been brought up. I think if I'm in a position to radically change other people's lives for the better, I should do so [...] I just want to live life to its full, you know, if I can make a difference, I hope to be able to make the difference. And I think one of the positive things at the moment is, you know, you've got Sergey and Larry from Google, for instance, who are good friends, and thank God, you've got two people who genuinely care about the world. And with that kind of wealth, if they had that kind of wealth and they didn't care about the world, it would be very worrying. And you know they're going to make a hell of a difference to the world. And I think it's important that people in that kind of position do make a difference." (Branson, 2007)

OPRAH WINFREY
Chairwoman, CEO, and CCO of the Oprah Winfrey Network

Raise your consciousness.

"There is an innate, supreme moment of destiny for everybody [...] and everybody has that. And you cannot fulfill it, unless you have a level of self-awareness, to be connected to what is the inner voice, or the instinct, I call it your emotional GPS system that allows you to make the best decisions for yourself. And every decision that has profited me has come from me, listening to that inner voice first, and every time I've gotten into a situation where I was in trouble, it's because I didn't listen to it. I overrode that voice, that instinct, with my own, with my own head, my own thinking. I tried to rationalize it, I tried to tell myself: 'but, you know, okay, you're going to make a lot of money, oh no...' And so, I am, I sit here, you know, profitable, successful, by all the definitions of the world. But, what really, really, really resonates deeply with me, is that I live a fantastic life. My inner life is really intact. I live from inside out. And everything that I have, I have because I let it be fueled by who I am, and what I realized my contributions to the planet could be. And my real contribution is it: looks like I am. I was a talk show host; it looks like. You know, I'm in the movies; it looks like. You know, I have a network. But my real contribution, the reason what I am here, is to help connect people to themselves, and the higher ideas of consciousness. I'm here to help raise consciousness. So my television platform was to help raise consciousness [...] I am gonna use television as a force [...] let's think about what we want to say to the world, and how we want to use this as a platform to speak to the world. How do we want to see the world change? [...] If there is a religion or mantra or law that I live by, I live by the third law of motion in physics which is: 'for every action there's an equal and opposite reaction' [...] I know that what I'm thinking and therefore gonna act on, is going to come back to me, in a circular motion [...] And so, what also propels the action is the intention. So, I don't do anything, without being fully clear, about why I intend to do it, because the intention, is going to determine the reaction, the result, or the consequence in every circumstance. I don't care what it is. So, I said to my producers, come to me with your intention [...] whatever ideas you're proposing, and then I will decide based upon the intention, do I really wanna do that? Is how we wanna use this platform [...] I come from a focus place, I come from compassion, it's just my nature, I come from a willingness to understand and to be understood, and I come from wanting to connect. I mean, the secret of that show for 25 years, is that people could see themselves in me, all over the world, they could see themselves in me. And even as I became more and more financially successful, which was a big surprise to me [...] but I realized is through the whole process, because I'm grounded in my own self, that although I can have more shoes, my feet stayed on the ground [...] and I can understand that it really was, because I was grounded, I was doing and continued to this day, to do the consciousness work. I work staying awake, and been awakened, is just another word for spirituality [...] everything is fueled that comes from me, really wanting to be a better person on earth. And this is what I know to be true, the reason why the show worked is because I understood that that audience, my viewers, and the people who watched us every day, and would come [...] all over the world, just to be there with their aunts, their mothers, and they'd come with their cousins [...] I had such regard for that. And I just had a conversation with John Mackey who runs Whole Foods [...] and he was talking about how the investment and stakeholders, the people who you are serving, that connection between the people who you are trying to serve and sell to, is equally as important as the people who you're buying from, equally as important as the people who supporting you financially [...] So, I always understood that there really was no difference between me and the audience, at times, I might have had better shoes. But at the core, the core of what really matters, that we are the same, you know how I know that? 'Cause all of us are seeking the same thing [...] everybody wants to fulfill the highest, truest expression of yourself as a human being. That's what you're looking for. The highest, truest expression of yourself as a human being. And because I understand that? I understand that, if you're working in a bakery, and that's where you want to be, and that maybe what you always wanted to do is to bake [...] then, that's for you, and there's no difference between you and me, except that's your platform, that's your show every day. So, my understanding of that, has allowed me to reach everyone. And there's no way that you wouldn't. Because that's what I truly feel [...] so, what I started to feel? Feel, sense. Is that there's a common thread that runs through every interview, it doesn't matter what is, or what it is about, and everybody wants to know. And this is the truth, all of your arguments are really about the same thing, it's about: Do you hear me? Do you see me? And, did what I say, mean anything to you? That's what everything's about […] so, having that understanding, and I would have to say that the show, one of the reasons why I live such a fantastic life, is because I pay attention; I pay attention to my life. And your life is your greatest teacher. Every single thing that's happening to you every day, your joys, your sadnesses, your challenges, your worries, everything is happening to bring you closer to in here. Everything is trying to take your home to yourself. And when you're home with yourself, when you're solidly there, connected to whatever you call creation, even if you don't call it anything, connected to an energy force that has unlimited power for you. You could connect to that. You are your best […] I knew that even though masses of people were not tuning in for that, that the whole purpose of that platform was to try to lift people up. And now I have a network, and I can articulate what it is I'm trying to do. I'm trying to bring little pieces of light into people's lives, because, what is my job? My job is not to be an interviewer; my job is not to be a talk show host or just to own a network, I am here to raise the level of consciousness, to connect people to ideas and stories, so that they can see themselves and live better lives […] You first have to change the way a person thinks and sees themselves, so, you've gotta create a sense of aspirations, a sense of hopefulness, so, a person can see, can begin to even have a vision for a better life. And if you can't connected that, then you lose and they lose, and it's just money after money after money […] you know, the light in my life was education, so for me, in the beginning, when I started to make money, especially when it's published, everybody, and your brother, calls you. And then you've got to make a decision: Am I going to do what everybody else wants me to do? Or, am I going to be led by who I really am? And I learned, as will happen to anybody who's successful in your family, people start treating you like the First National Bank. And you've got to decide. You've got to draw the boundaries for yourself. And decide, how are you gonna use your money, your talent, your time, in such a way that it's going to serve you first. Because if you, if it doesn't allow you to be filled up, then you get depleted and you no longer, you can't keep doing it. So my decisions are now emotional and logical. Meaning, I choose education, but I do it in such a way that's actually going to benefit the person that I'm serving. Then is not just, oh, I want to help people [...] But I always knew even during the show, that we live in a fame culture, we lived in a fame centered world, you know, had this literally been during the Renaissance, people would have valued different things, we've been doing the transcendentalist period, people valued different things, but in our culture we value fame. So I always understood that that was the basis for me being known in the world, because people wouldn't be able to hear you, unless you came with some swag or swagger, you know? And I also understood that that was just the foundation to be heard, but that there was a lot of more to be said. So for me, owning a network, or being a part of a network is about continuing to use that platform to raise the consciousness. I do a show [...] where I literally talk to thought leaders from around the world and ask the questions in life that really matter to get people thinking about what really matters in their lives and the responses that I get from people, just regarding that show, let me know that I'm on the right track, I'm moving in the right direction. And so, I'm not afraid, because I know that all of us have limited time here but the real question is: who are you? And, what do you want to do with it? And, who are you going to use who you are? [...] Align your personality with your purpose and nobody can touch you; and you wake up every day and you are fired up [...] because everybody has a purpose. So your whole thing is figure out what that is. You're real job is to figure out why you're really here and then get about the business of doing that. That's it [...] There are no mistakes. There really aren't any, because you have a supreme destiny. When you're in your little mind, in your little personality mind or you're not centered, you really don't know who you are, but you come from something greater and bigger. We really all are the same. If you don't know that, you get all flustered, you get stressed all the time, wanting something to be, what it isn't there's a supreme moment of destiny calling on your life. Your job is to feel that, to hear that, to know that. And sometimes, when you're not listening, you get taken off track. You get in the wrong marriage, the wrong relationship, you take the wrong job. But it's all leading to the same path. There are no wrong paths. There are none. There's no such thing as failure really, because failure is just that thing trying to move you in another direction. So you get as much for your losses, as you do from your victories, because your losses are there to wake you up [...] and ask yourself, what is the next right move? [...] and then from that space make the next right move, and the next right move, and not be overwhelming by, because you know your life is bigger than that one moment. You know you're not defined by what somebody says, is a failure for you, because failure is just the point you're in a different direction." (Winfrey, 2014)

LARRY PAGE
Co-Founder & CEO of Google

Follow your dreams.

"I want to talk about dreams for a second. And in my case, literally I dreamed. When I was in college, I was share, that I'd been in meaning by my clerical air: 'Prayer computer,' and because of that, I'd an irrational fear, might be sent home on the bus, and Sergei Sr. knows this is true, but it turns out causing that anxiety, I woke up, nearly when the dream was a kind of a strange dream. In one deck, I think I could download the entire web, and small computers there were lying around, and that poisoning pretty crazy of the most people. But I stayed up couple hours in the middle of the night, doing some math, and it seemed actually pretty possible. While zoom in action, we didn't keep any white beaches, they like kept to links, and then, turning figured out, given all that did I, I think that it had a couple weeks, and I told 'my visor' a lot, and he just had a lot to me, and of course took him a year too, as a year lot, we aren't, went to ranked white beaches, and no thoughts to search at all, and eventually search entered the picture, and you know the rest. And that became Google. So I want to create job one, to follow your dreams." (Page, 2013)

Pouring the Orange juice on business
Marketing

Who should ultimately design the product? The customer, of course
PHILIP KOTLER
American marketing author, consultant, and professor

As the second ingredient of the cocktail, their participation is to develop content that leave memory of your business. Its primary objective is to harmonize the active substance will enliven love for the brand in the market, with the aim of share their malleability to the demands and get the attention of the target market.

To get to know the word marketing is necessary to look at its origins.

According to Etimonline.com dictionary (2014) the *market* word comes from Latin *mercatus*, which means buying and selling, trading, market. Which served as the source for many languages including: *mercato* in Italian, *mercado* in Spanish, *markt* in German, for example. In Anglo Norman *marchiet* from Old French; were using to mean a meeting at a fixed time for buying and selling livestock and provisions in the old French market of northern; subsequently used as *marché* in modern French, and as *market* in the English, market or sell and trade, *marketing*.

According to Castillo & Bond (1987) the term *marketing* comes from the word *market* and the *ing* completion means effect an action.

In the sixties the Language Academy of Colombia proposed for adoption by *La Real Academia Española (RAE)* [The Royal Spanish Academy] (2012), which defines it as "a set of principles and practices that seek increased trade, especially increased demand."

Santesmases, Sanchez, & Valderrey (2003) mention that the term *marketing* has been consolidated in Spain and in some Spanish-speaking countries, so that the word *marketing* has a wide international recognition both academia and professionally. They add that although Mexico uses the translating *mercadotecnia,* today *marketing* has a widespread use, and not only applies to the company in exchange for economic, goods or services, but also in activities that are not for profit even ideas.

Marketing is a young discipline, with a very recent scientific development, characterized by multiple attempts to define and determine its nature and scope, which has resulted in numerous academic disputes, business and society, although marketing it is something that every day we hear more and applies to a greater extent, ignorance of what really is this discipline is still very significant.

So marketing is considered from different points of view:

1.   An academic discipline under study and research at the university.

2.   A professional discipline, application in business and other institutions that serve a market in particular and society in general.

3.   A philosophy because it is an attitude or way of thinking about the exchange relationship between a company that offers its products to market.

4.   A technique such as specific mode of carrying out the exchange relationship of identifying the gap, create and develop the object approach, to serve demand.

Butler (mentioned by Taylor & Shaw, 1990) defines it as how to put a product on the market considering and resolving many problems that go beyond considering selling, personnel takes just and advertising.

Santesmases et al. (2003) emphasizes that marketing has been used in various fields of study that has been given focus in different areas:

1.   Social Marketing: It serves the cause of non-governmental organizations with tools to make further donations and contributions, communicating their goals and results to the target audience, show through their management and invites people to collaborate.

2.   Noncommercial Marketing: Modifies behavior or attitudes of a segment of the population adapts to the mission and goals of a non-trading company to improve their situation, encouraging or discouraging social or cause social ideas.

3.   Marketing utility: Get closer between government service providers and their customers or citizens, according to the performance of official institutions that directly impact on improving the quality of life of the population.

4.   Political marketing: Cultivate the attention, interest and preference of the target market through a person's artistic, sporting and political arena

when it also puts in the market for votes in order to maximize your preference.

5.   Commercial Marketing: defines Fisher (1988) "is one that sells goods and / or services in an effort to gain economic profit."

According to Taylor & Shaw (1990) in most companies the marketing function is not fully developed due to various reasons:

1.   Recent origins of marketing: marketing is a relatively new commercial discipline and often confused with two of its sub-functions such as sales or advertising.

2.   Hostility towards marketing: strong vested interest in the company refuse to accept marketing and this must fight an uphill battle to establish their role, scope and authority.

3.   Law of slow learning: marketing goes through several stages of misunderstanding, as it grows in the company.

4.   Law quickly forgotten: marketing principles tend to be forgotten with the success and need to remember to executives with some regularity.

Santesmases, et al., (2003) allude to that marketing is a mindset, a philosophy of direction on how to understand the terms of trade of products and services of an organization with the market.

Basic Concept: The marketing process analyzes the selection of target market and product opportunities to develop the design with the marketing mix to achieve a successful business project.

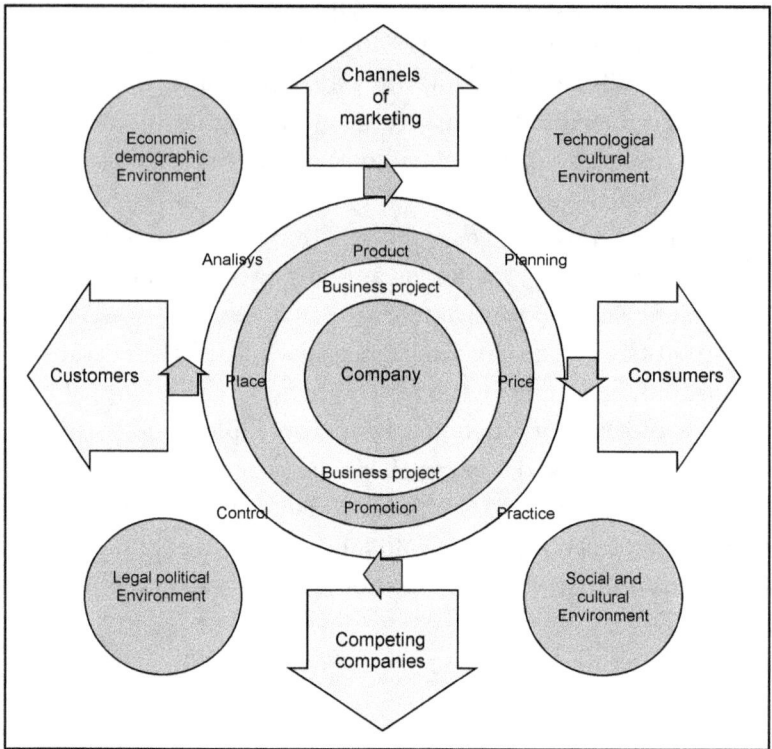

The marketing process and the factors influencing strategy of the company. Adapted from: Kotler, Philip; Amstrong, Gary. *Fundamentos de marketing.* [Principles of marketing] Mexico: Pearson Education, 2003. 589 pp. p. 49.

Marketing and consumer

Offer a customized product or service is one of the most effective ways to increase customer engagement
DON PEPPERS
American business executive, author and keynote speaker

To Santesmases et al., (2003) the trading activity or exchange of goods and services is one of the first who carried out the human being as he was associated with others of their species.

Taylor & Shaw (1990) argue that marketing goes back to the emergence of humanity and is considered one of the oldest professions in the world, this activity, with the passage of time and the increasing number and complexity of trade, has evolved much in the way of understanding and practice.

Stresses that marketing has evolved from its early origins in the distribution and sale into a whole philosophy aimed dynamically connect to any organization with its markets:

- 6000 years ago, the field of marketing is constituted. This is noted when humanity celebrates its first exchange, namely when two parties surplus resorted to barter as an alternative to own property.

- Barter evolved to the sale, which received high expression in very primitive civilizations.

- In the year of 1650, Japan's first member of the Mitzui family, is set in Tokyo as a trader and opened the first department store, anticipating 250 years to the policies of Sears by acting as a buyer for its customers, design products suitable for them and create sources for its production, the principle "is your money back no questions asked" and the idea of offering a variety of products to its customers.

- Around 1850 Cyrus H. McCormick clearly sees marketing as unique and central role of business enterprise, creating a customer as a particular task of management and gave the basics of modern marketing: market research and analysis, the concept of market position, pricing policies, vendor and customer service, spare parts supply and credit for the payment of subscriptions.

- In the early twentieth century marketing was first used in the United States but with a different meaning today. In those dates began to be taught in American universities courses on this new discipline and soon after, the first books were published.

- In the early 1900s the term "marketing" first appeared in collegiate titles.

- In 1905 W. E. Kreusi teaches a course at the University of Pennsylvania under the name of "Product Marketing."

- In 1910 Ralph Stan Butler offered a course entitled "Marketing Methods" at the University of Wisconsin.

- In 1911, the United States, the Curtis Publishing Company, installs the first marketing research department called "Commercial research."

- Santesmases et al., (2003) highlights that marketing began to penetrate the consciousness of different industries at different times. A few companies like General Electric, General Motors, Sears and Procter & Gamble, were among the first to realize their potential; this spread rapidly to companies of industrial products and consumer packaged goods.

- Coca Carasila (2008) says that in 1922 began to use radio signals as an advertising medium, and the first commercial arise in this area, which had an abysmal growth in just a decade.

- Were the universities that began to study the market and the influence of brands in people, but the global economic crisis in 1929 that followed during the decade of the 30, had devastating effects on rich and poor societies, people ran out employment, factories stopped production and marketing of products was relegated.

- In 1934 makes its appearance the American Marketing Journal, which from 1936 became the Journal of Marketing, and in 1937 the "American Marketing Association" (AMA) is created to promote the scientific study of marketing.

- The radio was the preferred mass media for advertising campaigns, until 1941 when advertising comes on TV.

- In 1945 comes the concern for the scientific content of marketing, As an example Converse (cited by Coca, 2008) in that year he published the article "The development of the Science of Marketing" in the Journal of Marketing, which can be considered as the beginning of the debate on the science of marketing.

• Early as 1950 Theodore Levitt introduces concepts such as target market and market segmentation, with the premise that advertising and sales efforts should be directed to the public that will be a potential customer for products, so begins the massive use of media communication for advertising purposes. The rise of television flourishes while the radio down, so do new strategies like telemarketing due to the large growth of households with telephone.

• From the 60s such limits are extended as in 1965, Ohio University defines marketing as the process by which a company anticipates, postponed or satisfies the demand structure of economic goods and services, through the conception , promotion, exchange and physical distribution of goods and services.

• Santesmases et al., (2003) notes that in 1969 Philip Kotler and Sydney Levy expanded the concept to include the marketing of non-profit institutions and public marketing, with products and customers, and perform activities such as those made in companies.

• In 1971 Philip Kotler and Gerald Zaltman, included social marketing aimed at influencing the acceptance of social ideas. In any case, it is the exchanges of (economic or otherwise) values benefit the parties to carry it out.

• Coca (2008) mentions that in 1983 according Wind and Robertson, constantly searched the integration between marketing and strategic planning, deriving in some integrative models.

• In 1984 Zeithaml & Zeithaml, declare that the focus of strategic marketing has a strong dose of proactivity with the environment, this vision is imperative conceiving it as a force that the organization can invoke to create change and expand its influence on the environment.

• That same year, Kotler (2009) defines marketing as a social and managerial process by which groups of individuals and organizations get what they want and need, through generating, providing and exchanging products with others.

• Fisher (1988) states that to engage in a social context both as a business, marketing is interested in consumer behavior where it operates not individually but according to environmental influences.

Basic concept: Success in global level business is only assured for those who maintain a solid understanding of its strategic responsibilities, disciplines that underpin and maturity of business diversification. (Adapted from Colmenares, 1992, Intro.)

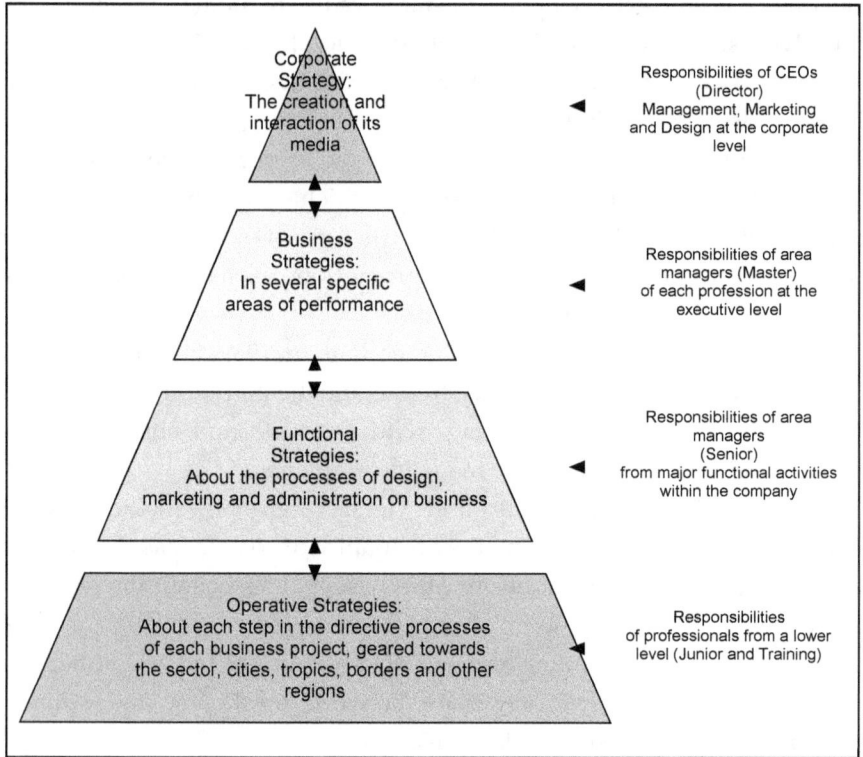

The Pyramid of the creation of the strategy in a company of diversified business. Adapted from: Thompson, Arthur; Strickland, A. J. *Strategic management. Concepts and cases.* USA: Mc Graw Hill, 2004. 398 pp. p. 53.

The aim of marketing

Make the brand experience exceeds the brand perception
STAN RAPP
American executive director of marketing and corporate cofounder

According to Schoell and Guiltinan (1991) in a society where free choice practiced when it comes necessary goods, whether products or services, the individual consumer desire becomes strategic. The cumulative force of the wishes of hundreds of millions of consumers in search of a satisfier is the enormous power that activates the marketer development.

Successful marketing is then achieved by selling products that satisfy this desire, anticipating those desires by offering their products; where consumers prefer to buy products that meet their desires in a maximum degree and minimum cost.

The most important characteristics of the current concept of marketing in which includes its position in business can be summarized in providing care to the consumer, however are not many organizations have, in fact, a consumer orientation, although declare that they apply marketing, all they do is, often, advertising or sale, without actually worrying about meeting the needs of potential customers.

So, is that marketing has been classified in various ways:

• Large sectors of society argue that marketing does not seek to meet the real needs of consumers, but creates those needs, and manipulates therefore the consumer is false the statement that "the customer comes first."

• Taylor & Shaw (1990) stress that sometimes marketing managers lose sight of their ultimate goals and focus on short-term gains or dubious benefit to themselves or others. When they lose that sense of higher purpose of marketing, their work becomes unsatisfactory and cynical.

• Schoell and Guiltinan (1991) comment that too, marketing is to organize and direct the use of resources, so that the income from sales of the product or service exceed costs and the surplus is maximized.

• This is, according to Taylor & Shaw (1990) maximizes consumption market whatever the company produces. But he adds that according to this point of view, the marketing manager is a technician who plans sales gains.

The current role of marketing in business does not always have the prominence it deserves.

Frías (2004) notes that erroneously academics and professionals have considered marketing as the art of selling products, but the goal of this discipline is not sales, is to know and understand customers well enough that the product or service generated no only meets the needs, but exceed them where possible, achieving this is sold almost alone.

In the words of Peter Drucker (mentioned by Taylor & Shaw 1990) "Marketing is so basic for business, it cannot be considered separately from a business function is the total enterprise from the perspective of its final outcome, i.e., from the standpoint of customer."

Taylor adds that during the last decades consumer service companies have opened and been input marketing. All large and small, from anywhere in the world, profit or nonprofit are beginning to appreciate the difference between sales and marketing and are organizing to carry out marketing.

In this sense, it is a fact that to effectively fill the effects of marketing in your business and your company, it is first necessary that you are aware of the need of its benefits, consequently assign a department or improve the functions plays and then administering professionally.

Schoell and Guiltinan (1991) comment that in the administration of marketing the masterful challenge is the change due to the growing quickly design innovations in products and services cause a constant pressure to adapt to the competitive market demands.

In this regard, attention should be given to four elements:

1.   Establish balance cost with satisfaction: To achieve maximum consumer preference as evenly as possible.

2.   Manage the market: In order to form satisfactory volume to the business and the consumer.

3.   Understand the nature of the market and part of the mechanical processes involving it towards the product and its effects on the consumer.

4.   Examine the changes occurred in marketing management in the long run to analyze the most important innovations that have been made.

When your company serves these points are involved aspects of marketing that are addressed the customer, giving a strategic sense the objective that both seek to fulfill, which is consummate satisfaction through exchanges of value.

Thus, we can define the strategic marketing in a larger context by analyzing market opportunities powerful and choose best positions following programs and controls created, supporting viable businesses and carrying the purpose and objectives of the company.

Taylor & Shaw (1990) emphasize that within organizations, the marketing department has the major responsibility to initiate the effort to create an attractive play opportunities for the company anywhere within the company from their products or services as well how to create, evaluate and select good ideas that are attractive as opportunities to the business environment:

1. The internal opportunities of the company: are movements of relevant marketing and these are suggested for the purpose, objectives, growth strategies and portfolio decisions of the company.

It is an attractive event relevant marketing action in which particular companies probably enjoy a differential advantage. Every company has distinctive competencies, namely things you can do especially well.

2. The environmental opportunities: are market possibilities of a company, while there are unmet needs.

In different industries there are great opportunities to create new and better methods for market but not necessarily represent an opportunity for some specific company. All environmental opportunity has specific requirements of success.

It is for this reason that the main technical contribution of strategic marketing is to evaluate the sales potential of each opportunity with useful methods to achieve serve the market.

By regard to Frías (2004) states that the objective of marketing in business fulfills the function of plan and create products and services enabling obtain a higher standard of living.

ARTIUX

Basic concept: In the process of marketing, the development of a new product requires an accurate communication to be useful, that excites the consumer and generates a higher standard of living.

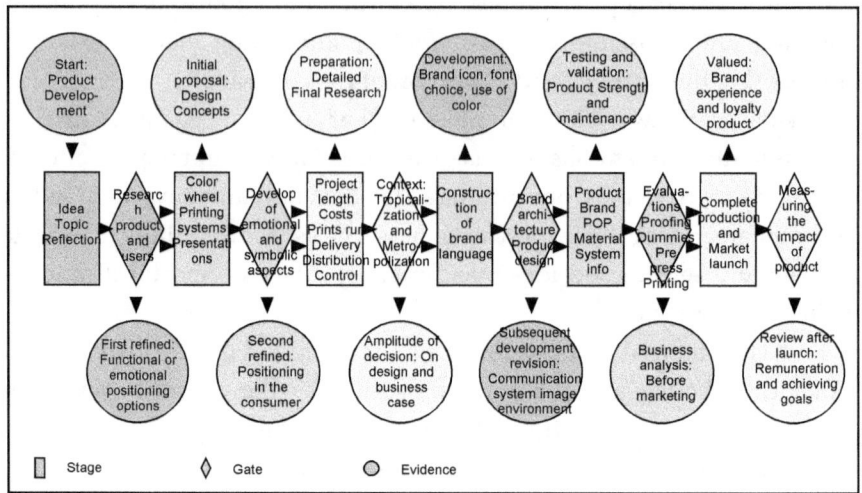

Gate stage system in developing a new product to market. Adapted from: Mullins, J.; Boyd, H.; Walker O.; Larreché, JC. *Administración de marketing. Un enfoque en la toma estratégica de decisiones.* [Marketing Management: A Strategic Decision-Making Approach] Mexico: Mc Graw Hill Interamericana, 2007, 519 pp. p. 258. And: Mono diseño; Charlotte Rivers; Clare Dowdy. *Identidad corporativa: del brief a la solución final. [Branding: From Brief to Finished Solution]* Barcelona: GG. Diseño, 2006, 158 pp. pp. 1&158.

The management of strategic marketing

If you think good design is expensive, you should look at the costs
of bad design
RALF SPETH
Important engineer and executive automotive German

For Lamb, Hair, & McDaniel (2011) marketing management is understood as designing activities related to the objectives and changes in the market environment.

Santesmases et al., (2003) propose that a director who plans marketing must make marketing decisions based on their judgment of the consumer response to cost-satisfaction aspects of products designed and supplying a company as well as in assessing its ability to educate that consumer response.

Munch (2009) notes that in large corporations, decision making effecting marketing managers are in charge of professional executives dedicated exclusively to the area where they also have specialists in their field. And in SMEs is rare to find companies with widely developed marketing departments.

The importance of the marketing department in a company focuses on gathering facts and factors influencing the market, to create what the consumer wants, desires and needs, distributing it so that it is available at the right time, in the right place at the most appropriate price.

To Enriquez (2013) the favorable point for the entrepreneur or small business owner is that the development of marketing strategy is not a fantasy that has to be associated with high costs; with the advancement in the electronic communication of content becomes relevant, since the cost generated It is really minimal.

In this sense Contreras (2001) states that the mission is an enduring statement of purpose of a company that distinguishes it from others and scope of operations of a company is in its products and markets.

So your mission statement must indicate the target characteristic that differentiates your company, in a unique way.

Kotler (2009) said that the mission statement is the expression of the purpose of the organization is, what you want to achieve in the wider environment. It also recommends that its construction is oriented towards the market, ie, in terms of meeting the needs of consumers.

Baena (2011) states that it is advisable that the mission statement is made on the market it has to serve, always careful not to fall into marketing myopia, which is to focus the business from a product perspective and not from the market.

In this tenor the most objective remuneration with which you can achieve consumer satisfaction is evaluating their opinion about a product or service requested or acquired for improvement. The marketing tool that manages the sole purpose of satisfying the needs of consumers it is the market study. This determines the factors that influence consumer buying decisions, ergo, analyzes their behavior on their site preferences market.

The American Marketing Association [AMA] (2004) defines market research as "function that links the consumer, customer and public to the seller through -used information to identify and define opportunities and marketing problems; generate, refine and evaluate marketing actions; monitor the performance of marketing; and improve understanding of marketing as a process-. Marketing research specifies the information required to address these issues, designs the method for collecting information, manages and executes the process of data collection, analysis of results, and communicates the findings and their implications."

Fisher (1988) says that when marketing analyzes the market environment, consumer preferences on a market or product are evaluated. According Fisher the market research relates to know who they are or may be consumers or potential customers to identify their characteristics.

Apply it can offer great benefits to your company based on their results, give better data to strengthen the tools of marketing management to increase product demand, the market share and profit.

Such tools are the 4 P's which together are called marketing mix, or product, price, promotion and place.

For the AMA (2014) the marketing mix is controllable variables that the firm uses to pursue the desired sales level in the target market.

Kotler & Amstrong (2003) defined as the 4 P's of the marketing mix:

1.   Product: The combination of goods and services that the company offers to the target market. Product design.

2.   Price: The amount of money that customers have to pay for the product. The product price.

3.   Promotion: Involves activities that communicate the benefits of the product and persuade target customers to buy it. The promotion that brings the product to the consumer.

4.   Place: Also known as distribution includes the activities of the company that makes the product will be available to target consumers. The place to exhibit and put in the hands of the consumer to the product.

These four elements are the basic tools of marketing director, which must base their decisions so that by combining offer benefits to the company.

The 4 variables are understood more clearly form when applied in market research:

1.   Knowing whether the consumer meets your needs or desires with the acquisition of the *product*.

2.   Knowing if the consumer is satisfied with the *price* or considers money to pay is greater than the benefit obtained.

3.   Knowing the details of the means of *promotion* in greater impact or influence it has had on the consumer.

4.   Knowing lastly if the consumer buys your product in the distribution site or *place* at the right time.

Against the background described each P will create its strategy:

1.   For the product: its value added, scilicet, render our products in a higher than our competitor idea.

2.   For the price, that can be modified, from being diminished by the low cost production to offer attractive discounts to return the product purchase.

3.   To promote: the media or ideas expressed our message to the consumer, the more concrete and attractive the more favorable communication will result.

4.   For the place: choosing the right place to carry out the distribution, a relationship between the company expanded its market to bring the product to the customer.

It is important to remember that the implementation of the marketing mix should be based on market research, taking into account competition and trends, to provide the bases and tools needed on the profitability of the strategy is generated.

Faced with the responsibility of the strategy work, every marketing effort should be linked to what is meant by Lamb, Hair, & McDaniel (2011) argue that introducing situational analysis better known as SWOT, identification of internal and external environment is determined in which the sale of the product or service is performed.

Basic Concept: The proper conformation of the strategy begins with the identification of opportunities and risks in the external environment to put into action opportunities with company resources to implement the strategy.

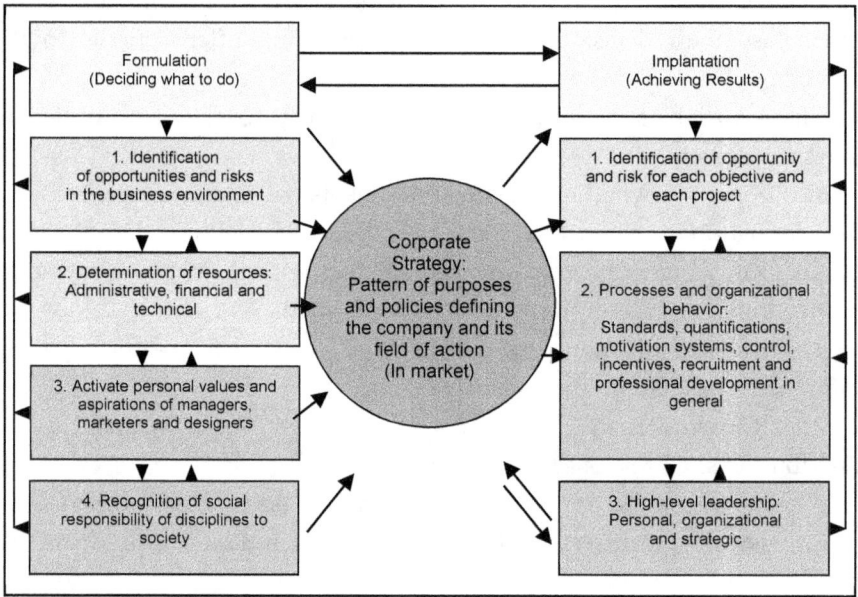

The implementation of the strategy in a company. Adapted from: Mintzberg, Henry; J. Brian; J. Voyer. *El proceso estratégico. Conceptos, contextos y casos*. [The strategic process. Concepts, contexts and cases]. Mexico: Prentice Hall Hispanoamericana, 1997. 641 pp. p. 54.

The marketing planning

You have to live with your product. You must imbibe it. You have to saturate of it. You must get to the heart of it. Yes, but if there is not an original concept that can be communicated to the reader, you cannot be creative
WILLIAM BERNBACH
American advertising creative director

In a business environment where debated by the market both retail and wholesale large scale, gain an advantage that allows them to compete better is the crucial basis for strategic marketing why, is based on planning. The marketing department uses the marketing plan as an essential tool for operation.

Enriquez (2013) says that a large corporation or a small business looking to compete successfully in marketing their products or services, should plan and establish four initial marketing tactics:

1.   Create an unmistakable brand identity: Business success is determined by its powerful ability to communicate accurately and provide a defined, simple and consistent experience. In short it is called making "branding," and when done right, it ensures a business in the minds of customers that the company needs. The brand identity should be strong, clear, and created before any other action marketing.

2.   Identify the target audience to connect with him: What the company has to offer, someone specific wants and needs. And this is not everyone. The target is only those people who need it, and exactly, those who are willing to pay for it. Identify well the specific group of consumers having characteristics in times, places and special circumstances, will unveil a connection to attract them.

3.   Generate compelling offers to attract customers like a magnet: It is working on providing customers what excites them and want to feel, to arrive visualize how these services can meet these feelings. The customer wants to know "What's that to me?" Enter the feeling and create offers that excite their customers. Make them their delirious fans. All buying decisions are based on emotion and feeling.

4.   Land achievable marketing plan: Do everything required for the product or service becomes available, more convenient and more

profitable. The marketing plan should set the overview to provide a comprehensive approach basing on the client. Developing a plan automatically achieve an advantage over most of the competition, provided that this is objective and feasible to achieve business goals.

Properly implement marketing planning can transform any business large or small, in a commercial strength that can extend its scope, with satisfied customers. Its flexibility and dynamism depend largely on the accuracy of the initial work to develop your content.

Sanz de la Tajada, (mentioned in Sainz de Vicuna, 2013) states that the marketing plan is a written document in which a systematic and structured way, anticipated the corresponding analyzes and studies, defining objectives to be achieved in a period of time, as well as programs and means of action to be accurate detailing to achieve the stated objectives within the period expected.

Both (Fischer & Espejo, 2004) and (Stanton, Etzel, & Walker, 2007) suggest that it should draft a document for planning marketing efforts and work throughout the company, this is the strategic marketing plan that develops six major steps:

Stanton et al., (2007) agree:

1.   Situational analysis: Where a SWOT analysis as a diagnostic is included, consumer groups who are directed the company, strategies to satisfy them and the principal measures of performance marketing. It also identifies and evaluates competitors that address the same markets.

2.   Objectives of marketing: They keep a close relationship with corporate goals and strategies. Each objective should receive priority regarding their demands, their results in the area and their preponderance in the organization. Then, resources must be allocated according to these priorities.

3.   Positioning and Differential advantage: The positioning is the result of the preference of the product against competing products in the market and with other products in the same company. The differential advantage will any feature of an organization or brand that consumers perceive desirable and distinct against competition.

4.   Target market and Market demand: Are the target groups of people or organizations to which the company focus its marketing efforts. Then, it includes a forecast of demand, or sales in the target markets that

seem most promising to consider and decide the appropriate segment or alternative.

5. Mix marketing: is the combination of many aspects of the following four elements: which product is, what its price, how it is promoted and where it distributes. The role of each of these elements is to satisfy the target market and fulfill marketing objectives of the company.

Fischer & Espejo (2004) project also:

6. Evaluation of results or Control: The tool that will constantly monitor and evaluate each operation of the strategic marketing plan for the end result adheres as closely as possible to the desired.

They add that the advantages of planning favor to:

a) Encourage the systematic thinking of marketing management.

b) Improve coordination of all activities of the company.

c) To guide the organization regarding objectives, policies and strategies that must be carried out.

d) Avoid that there are surprising developments within the activities of the entire company.

e) Contribute to have greater participation of executives, to interrelate their responsibilities to changes in company projects and the setting in which it operates.

Taylor & Shaw (1990) say that the main contribution of strategic marketing is to evaluate the sales potential of each opportunity with useful methods to achieve serve the market.

Lamb et al., (2011) point out that the relationship between marketing and strategic planning requires the proper focus of the marketing plan. The decisions that the director of marketing department should do in this plan are inescapable interest of the company.

According to Lamb, decision making is part of the strategic direction, is performed taking into account the benefits that the organization expects in a given period and is based on the matrix product / market, also called Ansoff box. It is a technique for analyzing business that identifies growth opportunities. It may help to consider the implications of business growth through products and markets, traditional or new. Each of these growth options is based on research, influence and internal and external analysis, then work on the strategy chosen.

According to Free-management-ebooks.com (2013) maintains four marketing strategies, the sequence is:

1. Market penetration: Focusing your sales of existing products or services to your existing markets and achieves growth in market share.

2. Market development: Focus on developing new markets or market segments for your existing products or services. Promotes demand.

3. Product Development: Focus on new developments of products or services to your existing markets. Active frequency.

4. Diversification: Focusing on the development of new products or services for sale in new markets.

To plan the market is necessary market research that you used to collect your representative sample, the necessary data which require converted into the product want to get your target audience.

Basic Concept: The process of planning and executing of a market research has stages that can be understood as a cyclical process, as the research findings presented generate new ideas or new problems amenable to research.

I. DESIGN
1. FORMULATION OF THE PROBLEM: Just posing it properly finds the right answer.
1.1 Discovery: • Discover the existing need to solve. • Value the opportunity. For example, introducing a new product in the range. • Evaluate the strategy adopted by the business address.
1.2. Definition: • Define precise objectives to guide entire process that follows. • It raises the questions or hypotheses that research must solve or contrast. • Answer the question: "Why do we do this research?" • Define an idea of the information needed and how to obtain it.
2. DETERMINATION OF RESEARCH DESIGN: Tackle the problem and its nature.
2.1 Exploratory Design: • Use secondary information sources and qualitative research methods based on small (group dynamics, depth interviews observation, and so on.) samples. • Identify threats and opportunities in the environment. • Define the problems precisely at the level of objectives and questions. • Raises hypotheses explaining the facts to identify basic variables and their possible relationships.
2.2 Conclusively Design: • Contrast the hypotheses formulated after performing an exploratory investigation. • Evaluate and select action alternatives. • Establish relationships between the variables of interest.
2.2.1 Descriptive Design: • Research by surveys, obtaining samples that allow generalizing the results to the population. • Respond to questions: "who," "what," "when," "how much," "how," "where," and "why," quantitatively. • Describe and measure market phenomena that occur frequently. • Determines the degree of association between variables. • Make predictions.
2.2.2 Causal Design: • Estimate how far changes in one variable (controllable independently or treatment) produces changes in other variables (uncontrollable, dependent or effect) in a temporal sequence. • Identify and specify fully the research problem. • Determine which variables or treatments are independent and what the dependent. • Determine the functional relationships between causes and effects. • Its methodology is the experimental method. Controls the external conditions so that one or more variables can be manipulated to test a hypothesis about how it affects another, and all this is usually performed using control groups.
3. PREPARATION: Delimits all previous fieldwork activities.
3.1. Determination of the required information: • Secondary information is that which already exists, is prepared and published. It may have been generated by the company itself or by third parties and can dispose of it because they were stored in the company (internal) itself, or outside (external). The latter can be bibliographical or obtained for free (publications and databases in libraries of public schools), or can be syndicated, or acquired for a price to companies specialized in obtaining information. • The primary information is collected specifically for the research question being addressed because the necessary information has not been previously collected by anyone or you do not have access to it. Therefore, it must be generated through qualitative research (group dynamics, interviews, observation, projective techniques) or quantitative (surveys, experiments, observation).
3.2. Determination of the method of obtaining: • For qualitative techniques such as group dynamics, in-depth interviews, projective techniques or direct observation. These techniques are very flexible; they lack rigid structures and include, typically, a few sample elements (respondents). Allow exploration of the issues and the presentation of hypotheses. • For quantitative techniques: as survey research, direct observation and experiment design. These techniques typically involve the use of structured questionnaires and include a large number of respondents, as they require that the results can be projected to the population. When to confront the research problem is sufficient to obtain secondary information, this subphase will be reduced to the determination of their sources of information, which will take the form of available publications and databases.
3.3. Designing the questionnaire: • The questionnaire is the formal instrument or medium customarily used for collecting reliable and valid primary information. Generally a good questionnaire will be enjoyable and easy to complete. • Gets primary information involves performing a series of special activities such as questionnaire design and the test sample. • Decide assessment scales to be used to measure the variables of interest. So, we will have to choose between comparative or not comparative scales; between scales of a single item or multi-item, ... • Determine the structure (order or sequence of questions) and format (of great importance in self-administered questionnaires). • Make a previous test of it with a small subsample in order to improve before final application.
3.4. Sample design: • The sample is a subset of the population in general representation selected for study. Individuals, households, businesses, ... • Ensures the representativeness of selection, so that the study results can be generalized to the population. • Define the purpose of the study population and identified by a sampling frame. • Determines the method for selecting the elements of the sample from the sampling frame (probability or non-probability) that decisively affects the degree of representativeness of the sample. • Decide on the sample size, aspect that affects the precision of the estimates and the cost of the study. From the set size can be estimated sampling error of the estimates.
II. SEARCH

4. FIELD WORK: Collect information with the questionnaire.
4.1. Planning: organization and programming of field work, including preparation of instructions; they must be set the rules concerning how to select interviewees (when and where to select the sample).
4.2. Preparation of interviewers: Includes selection and training. It is intended that interviewers are familiar with a series of general rules and the specific research in which will help. This phase involves the development of a set of instructions on the correct application of the questionnaire and instructions for each of the questions in the questionnaire.
4.3. Conducting interviews: Involves the actual selection of sampling units and conducting the survey. That is, it is the field work itself.
4.4. Control of work: Involves the supervision of surveys conducted by interviewers.

III. ANALYSIS

5. INFORMATION PROCESSING: Give precisely riverbed information obtained.
5.1. Edition: It consists in reviewing the questionnaires received from the field to decide whether they are valid for analysis. The edition involves examining various aspects, some directly on the paper questionnaire and other later (for verification) on the computer support, once the data has been recorded.
The edition leads to the exclusion of those questionnaires that do not meet the minimum quality established by decreasing the size of the sample. Represents a process of controlling the work of interviewers.
The following aspects are discussed mainly:
• No missing pages in the questionnaire.
• That key survey questions have been answered.
• That key survey questions are answered correctly, that is, following the instructions provided.
• That the questionnaire was answered by individuals in the target population.
• That has been completed sample quotas.
In addition, it is also very important to check the following points:
• The consistency in the answers of respondents. For this control questions included in the questionnaire are analyzed. For example, it is not consistent one respondent stating that no known specific brand, but later claims to have ever bought.
• The interviewer does not influence the respondent's answers. To do all questionnaires from the same pollster as a whole are reviewed to determine that no suspicious patterns of response are observed.
• The no falsification of questionnaires by the interviewer. For this makes so-called endorsement, it consists in to call a percentage of respondents to verify that the questionnaire was done actually and effectively.
5.2. Encryption: consists of assigning codes (usually numeric) to each of the response options for each question. This facilitates the recording of data and statistical analysis of the responses from the sample by software. This process usually develops during the design phase of the questionnaire, since it is highly desirable that the codes assigned to each question and answer option appear in the questionnaire to facilitate the process of recording the data to the computer file.
5.3. Designing the database: It consists in designing the structure of the file that will contain all the raw data obtained in the field of research. Essentially involves creating variables that represent the concepts measured by the questionnaire. This process also should do it as part of questionnaire design.
5.4. Recording: This involves the transcription of data from paper support (questionnaire) to the computer database prepared. After recording the data, the file contains the coded answers given by all respondents to the questionnaire.
5.5. Verification: This involves a process of editing the recorded data. It is found that the recording contains no errors and that the questionnaires gather maximum quality (coherent answers, no influence of the interviewer...).
6. TABULATION AND ANALYSIS: These sub-phases of the entire process.
6.1 Tabulation: The objective is the initial exploration of the obtaining data, providing the basic results. It involves counting and summarizing ordered arrangement of raw data (stored in the file) in a table or other summary format. Equivalent to calculating the frequency distribution of each variable, that is, the count of absolute and relative frequencies each answer choice for each question.
6.2 Analysis: It involves the development of different operations on the raw data, beyond the simple count, in order to get results and conclusions not directly observables, namely not derived from simple observation of the frequency tables. Allow to simplify the information collected with the survey or contained in the data file and draw conclusions about the behavior of the variables. The analysis can be:
• Descriptive: if the objective is to summarize the information from the sample. Descriptive statistics (means, variances, correlations ...) are used.
• Inference: if the goal is to make judgments about the behavior of the population based on the results of the sample. Inferential statistical techniques (test or hypothesis contrasts) are used.
Furthermore, depending on the number of variables analyzed simultaneously, the analysis can be:
• Univariate: if each variable is studied separately (mean, variance ...).
• Bivariate: if relations between pairs of variables (correlation, cross tabulation ...) are analyzed.
• Multivariate: if more than two variables are analyzed simultaneously. Multivariate methods are characterized by their great potential for treatment and simplification of data. The most widely used in market research are the following: correspondence of factorial analysis, principal component analysis, classification analysis (cluster), multidimensional scaling analysis, discriminate analysis, regression analysis, analysis of joint actions (conjoint) analysis of variance and hierarchical segmentation analysis.
Finally, the level of measurement of variables in order to select the most suitable type for data analysis should also be considered. In this sense must differentiate between metric and non-metric data (either ordinal or nominal).

IV. COMMUNICATION OF THE REPORT

7. COMMUNICATION AND PRESENTATION
7.1 Written report and oral presentation: The formal drafting supported in a speech for their projection. As the unique aspects of the study that will know the marketing manager, their assessment will depend largely on the way in which is communicated.
• Include the beginning of the report a short summary called 'executive', in a couple of pages summarizes the most relevant from research.
• Start the speech with the target and always be brief, but thorough.
• Include at least the nature of the research problem and research objectives.
• Applied Methodology (consulted sources of information, methods of obtaining information applied, sample selection, analysis techniques used ...).
• Results obtained.
• Conclusions and recommendations.

Stages of process of market research. Adapted from: EducaMarketing (2005) *Guía para realizar una Investigación de Mercados* [A guide for develop a Market Research] Extremadura, Spain: University of Extremadura.

Competitiveness

The essence of competitiveness is liberated when we make people believe what they think and do is important and then get out of their way while they do
JACK WELCH
American business executive, author and chemical engineer

To Wikipedia.org (2015), the concept of competitiveness is understood as the ability to generate greater customer satisfaction by offering the association of a lower price compared to some quality; the most competitive companies will take more market share at the expense of less competitive businesses if there are not market failures that prevent it.

The loss of competitiveness describes an increase in production costs, as this will adversely affect the price or profit margin without providing improvements to product quality.

To assimilate the importance of competitiveness and make it work to the business environment need to understand what Porter (1990) considered the basic unit of analysis to understand business competition, is the sector, the business entity where interact a group of competitors who manufacture products or provide services and compete directly with each other.

Porter (1980) said that there, the nature of competition consists of five competitive forces:

1.   The bargaining power of buyers: The powerful clients are able to capture more value if they force down prices, demand better quality or better services which increases costs and generally make participants sector confronted; all this at the expense of industry profitability, especially if they are price sensitive and primarily use their power to press for price reductions.

2.   The bargaining power of suppliers: Powerful providers capture a greater share of value for themselves by charging high prices, restricting the quality or services, or transferring costs to industry participants. When a global corporate hike rates additions to a product, contributes to erosion profitability for the other manufacturers of the same product that have very limited possibilities to raise their prices.

3.   The threat of new entrants: New entrants in a sector introduce new capabilities, and a desire to gain market share, putting pressure on prices, costs and the rate of investment needed to compete. They can leverage existing capabilities and cash flows to shake the competition, especially when diversify from other markets. The threat of new entrants, therefore, places limits on the profitability potential of a sector.

4.   The threat of substitute products or services: A substitute performs the same or a similar function as the product of a sector through various forms. The video conferences are a substitute for travel. Plastic is a substitute for aluminum. The e-mail is a substitute for express mail. Also when a substitute replaces the product of a buyer sector. The sale of turf is threatened when multifamily buildings crowd the suburbs; or when the websites of airlines substitute for travel agents.

5.   The rivalry among existing competitors: This rivalry takes many familiar forms, including price discounts, new products, advertising campaigns and service improvements. A high degree of rivalry limits the profitability of the sector. The degree to which the rivalry reduces profits of an industry depends primarily on the intensity with which companies compete and, secondly, of the basis on which they compete.

Each of these competitive forces reacts according to their intensity within the structure of the sector and this influence companies to choose a position within the same.

Porter adds that the center position is the competitive advantage, which develops two main strategies for competitiveness:

1.   Focus on lower cost or overall cost leadership: It is determined by the ability of a company to design, fabricate or make and to market the products or comparable services more efficiently than its competitors at a low cost.

2.   Focus on differentiation or Differentiation wide: The ability to provide the buyer with a particular product or service superior value with the advantage of being singular in terms of quality, physical characteristics and visual qualities that make it unique and special.

Kotler & Armstrong (2003) allude that have a competitive advantage when competing with companies in the same industry where customer loyalty is won or has any superiority gained by offering consumers greater value than the offered by competitors.

In this sense, Kotler says that the competitive advantage of low costs translates to a reduction in costs as a result of the acquisition of low-cost raw materials, contribution or donation of material for the company or production technology conditions capable of reducing these. The advantage of low cost does not mean that quality is lousy compared to products made with materials more expensive. The intent of this strategy is to sell a product or service at a lower price than the competition.

Lamb et al. (2011) notes that the competitive advantage of differentiation is to add a quality that can be attended by the target market as unique in the market. This attention by the market influences such that the product price moves to a secondary importance. Differentiation can be seen as the inclusion of new applications, technologies or tools to a product.

This advantage should be applied a specific market segmentation serving only a group of people with similar characteristics.

The company must maintain its competitive advantage as long as possible as one of their strategies. Competitive advantage is, "the advantage that the competition cannot copy" and will be renewed when competition achieves copy the differentiating strategy.

Porter (1990) says that to gain a competitive advantage required a set of ideas that are not present in many companies. Most of companies value stability and no change. His constant concern is to protect ideas and old techniques, not create new ones.

In that sense, Mintzberg, et al. (1997) highlights the strategists who want to design their organizations to be efficient using all the resources at their disposal with well-defined parameters. Emphasizes differentiation strategy that relates to offer something that really is different; supported in design, this tries to break with the dominant design, if it exists, and provide unique features.

That is to have emerged new strategies to fortify the competitiveness of enterprises.

Lawrence (1996) express that it is amazing how is that design is still unknown and so misunderstood among entrepreneurs, despite looking for with dire need any potential competitive advantage.

Filson & Lewis (2000) point out that SMEs tend not normally use the design as a significant source of business, which may specifically be due to ignorance of its benefits.

So is that Olson, Slater, & Cooper (2000) assert that exist at the center of any competitive business strategy a set of differentiating competencies that are the resource holding the advantage of the company. A valuable strategy that is increasingly known, but it is still largely ignored as a resource to obtain this advantage is the design.

Basic concept: To manage differentially in the market, will should be recognized to design as an important resource of business and run their specific strategies to the sector in which it competes.

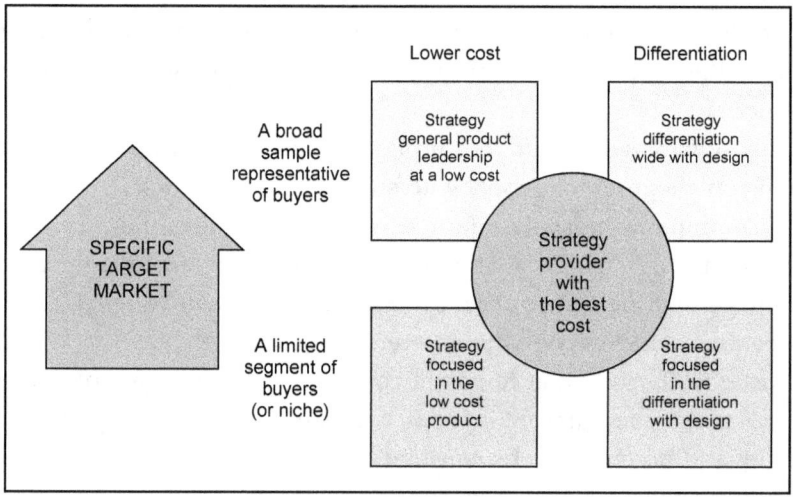

The five generic competitive strategies. Adapted from: Porter, Michael E. *Competitive Strategy*. New York: Free Press, 1980. 407 pp. p. 153.

These 6 behaviors of the marketing correspond to the Orange. Use them to project the love of your company and share the high values of consciousness that passionate people.
Make them fall in love with what they memorize of your company

The ice on background | PART 2
Pervading Orange

There are essentially two things that will make you wise, the books you read and the people you meet
JACK CANFIELD
American author and motivational speaker

PHIL KNIGHT
Co-founder & chairman of Nike

Listen your inner voice.

"I graduated from the school in 1962 more than half a century ago, was a time when jet travel have just beginning with the introduction of the Boeing 707, there was no Sillicon Valley per se, there were no 'spacks' machines, there was no internet, there were no cell phones, no iPads, the latest technological development was the color TV, there was no such thing as bencher capital, the number one company in the world was General Motors, the biggest firm on Wall Street was Merril Lynch Pierce Fenner & Smith, commercial banks we're not allowed to engage an investment banking activities, and there was no birth control pill up. There's absolutely nothing on my journey that has any specific application for what awaits you, in so many ways today's talk could be called 'return at the dinosaur.' Therefore, why, before this, the greatest class ever to graduate, from this: Best Business School on the planet, why did the dean asked me to be here? And my answer is, that I already know. But I suppose there may be some hope, the parts of my journey might be relevant on attitude and philosophy, I hope so. But, why I, a person who intensely disliked public speaking, choose to accept? Is perfectly clear to me, the answer is, it is personal, for me is around in a gird circle, there's a part of me that was born in you. I'd come here at age 22 a bit lost, for me an extrovert, was a person who spared at other people's shoes. Shy, insecure, and sure what I want to do with my life. Two years later I left, much better educated I was still shy and insecure, but I knew what I wanted to do if only I could put it off. And that was to bring to life the business plan, written in, French shad, and burgers, and entrepreneurship class. So I return 52 years after my own graduation to this place, this magical place which is extended part of me, I returned to say: Thank you here, for all the aspiration, again. In the summer between my first and second year, I'd had a long existential debate with myself, finally concluding that I would before going to work for forty years, take one year to go around the world looking for education, for enlightenment, looking for myself. And in the winter term of my second year, I took that entrepreneurship class whose road let me to Japan. So, after putting in my required two weeks US Army's, aren't capped at for odd, selling my car, saying bluntly honest parents and two sisters, I shut up with Gary Carter, who I met, on we're both living including's all. September we're ready to go, we trotted down to 'El Camino,' to the liquor store, was the ticket agent for Standard Airways, a discount charter airline. For eighty dollars we got on a 'Condor Air A,' a prop of force, leading from Moffet Field, eight hours airway. We would surf in the mornings and sell encyclopedias door to door in the evening. I'm sure I am the only graduate in the history of this school, whose first job after graduation, was selling encyclopedias. After a month to this, I was ready to go on, but Gary had met a girl, like the little too much to leave. So now I'm stuck with the decision, go home, or not go at all. I loved Japan instantly; the people are friendly in many parts of the countryside scenic. And the endless three sixty little dollar, so, so, many things were affordable, like hotel rooms, and meals, and athletic shoes. After a week I ran my way to Kobe, which was the headquarters benefits of the Company limited, manufactured Tiger athletic shoes, which I identified as the best quality, the one to the best chance, of getting a piece of the US market. I called in a telephone, and explain that I was a US businessman in town, and I had an interest in distributing their shoes in United States. I got an appointment. I'd on my one business suit, 'Brooks brothers,' with blue oxford shirt, black necktie, slipped on my blackberry loafers, and took a taxi, so, the wrong location, 'good ridge science.' I had gone to the showroom, they, one-minute manufactured with facility, completely, on the other side of town. So I show up a half hour late, I already nervous, and even know that is was a cool day, I was sweaty heavily. I met at the door by 30's man, Ken Miyazaki, who reach me warmly and assist me through to a conference room in the back of the building. On the way to the room, would pass through the accounting department, which has about 20 employees, they all stand up and bout, on the big businessman from the US you know. My entire asset throughout my body, that business suit, and my round the world airline check. That occurred to me, that I mind I got older alive. The half dozen Japanese businessmen wearing the conference room, how does the shy and insecure person, making a sales presentation, sell as if your life depended on it, budget sordid then by. For a mass context, when I said I sold encyclopedias door to door in Honolulu, was a little imprecise. I called on how is the door to door, trying to sell encyclopedias, and I never actually close a sale. After a very awkward beginning, we got into specifics about what was needed for the US market, the talks warm up and eventually become enthusiastic. They've been thinking about getting into the US market, and had several track and field sample model, built on parents of the US food, they were an all-purpose model, like all the limper up. The high jump model, could spring up, and not to discuss you, they called: the throw up. I might be able to help them. So we end with me, placing and order 15 pair samples, and after I leave, as alone and sharing a chaotic Osaka airport, and ask myself again, where am I going? I'm very excited about the meaning within its Co. And one part says, 'this is exactly what I want.' I sure rays sun and get this business going. The other said, 'If you don't go around the world now, you not go for five decades.' I flew to Hong Kong, which is a good thing; the samples had been rife reporting much. When the samples finally came, and I show in the mail-coach Bill Bowerman, who was so impressed, a young man on the deal, we shock hands on a 50-50 partnership, and each must put up five hundred dollars. We bought three hundred pair shoes. First year sales were eight thousand dollars, limited to 150 of profit. In 1964 my life got busy, by day I was the CPA for PriceWaterHouse, my army reserve requirement takes up two Tuesday night a month, and one all-day Sunday, plus two weeks in the summer. Dating with mix success, and all of was my real love, was that little company that Bowerman and I've started. We get two hundred thousand dollars in sales. We get the 500,000; then a million. I multitask. I can drive a car in the McDonald's, filet-a-fish decks, and reading a newspaper, all at

the same time. I was pretty efficient for a couple years, until I rear ended
the car in front of me. Took a lot of time, to get insurance companies lined
up my own car, repaired, and the cuts on my forehead fixed. So I don't do
anymore. By 1972 we got the two million dollars in sales, with the three
percent net profit, but it hadn't been easy; after all, five hundred dollars
apiece, doesn't provide much equity, even for two million dollars. I trust
in most my PriceWaterHouse check for four years, but I spending four
days a week at the bank trying to convince them to give us a little more
credit. By now I quit PriceWaterHouse and I'm going full time. In
somewhere in the process, my search for credit put me in touch with
Nissho Iwai, the six largest Japanese Trading Company, with annual sales
of $100 billion dollars. We began developing a positive relationship,
meanwhile and it is ok, had brought 32 year old hotshot, Shoji Khatami.
To the charge, to expand export sales; export sales were primarily us. So
youngster Khatami bring be the following offer: sell a 51 percent of your
company at book value, all set up other distributors, regardless what that
piece of paper that we sign says. With Khatami's ultimatum, I didn't
instant cost-benefit analysis, which let me to this dilemma: How do you
say go to the hell in Japanese? So there I am 34 years old, married, a 3 years
old son, eighty percent mortgage on my house, 45 employees, the personal
guarantee the seven hundred fifty thousand dollar company loan, and
enjoy going more obsolete by the day, and no new product to sell. We are
a team that are taken, that have been nothing eight years before, and built
it up, to become recognized in sporting goods world, and that team, that
designed the three top selling Tiger running shoes. We had a large pot of
coffee, and the support the six largest Japanese trading company. And that
trading company, could and did, introduce us to every shoe factory in
Japan, and provided the financing to import those products; but then there
was the little matter the lawsuits. Plural, one in the US, one in Japan. I get
my cousin, dog house of Stanford law 1960, to take our case on a
contingency, it took three years. We won both suits. Meanwhile we paid
$35 dollars to a graphic artist, too net poured in State College, to give a
rendition aside laureate in the shoe, the law now call it the 'swoosh'. Years
later, she was interviewed by the Portland Oregon announcement: 'what
are second biggest project was?' she answered, 'wallpaper for a wall a wall
a motel.' Read each the 45 employ submits a suggestion for a brand name,
Jeff Johnson, 1963 Stanford Graduate, wide mid-on workout an angle field,

and who was our first employed, summited the name Nike. Well, I said, don't really like it that much, but it's better than the other 44, and hope fully up grows. We were no longer limited to track a field shoes, so we bought n' brought in wrestling shoes, tennis shoes, basketball shoes as well, and sales grew 3.2 million dollars, but we had our first ever loss, plus one other problem, got kicked out of our bank. Too much leverage not enough cash. State Oregon only had two big banks and we've been thrown out the other 12 years before, the show we watched it in, for the bank, until we found one, the first date bank to Milwaukee area, a small bank, but we made it work. So there, I was sitting at my desk more relax than any time, and more than a decade, in the period between getting cut off by Tiger in establishing a banking relationship with First State Bank of Milwaukee and Oregon, sales, million, through the introduction of the running shoe with the waffle sole, risen to try five million dollars with solid profitability, oh yes, but it up in the morning mail letter has says: 'United States Customs. We announcement that this is an important letter ...' it turned out to be saw, attach was an invoice for past two customs duties of $25 million dollars, the exact same number as our total sales for the year. I had no idea what they talking about, so what we find out, this is a little use part of the Customs Code dating back to nineteen thirties, duty in three categories: mentoring chemicals, cherry stone clams, and athletic foot wear in a synthetic uppers; could be assessed not the factory cost of the goods, but in America whole sale, selling price for those goods, if in fact, goods were like, or similar, for like that language to American manufactured goods. So here comes this invoice, and despite the fact that we've been charging paid the amount that we had been invoiced for previously, our prices have been based on that, and long ago been sold. The $25 million dollars was on top of that. But things were buzzing in clear, one thing was absolutely certain; no way, we're going to be able to pay that amount of money. So, to go to Washington DC, reaching as high up in the political ladder as I can, and first contemplating imported nylon, up a running shoes weird, as customs for ruling on what to do we would be; when shown the letter signed by the assistant director custom, sitting, arguably 20 percent at factor cost, not the double that, that we are being assessed responsive John P. Simpson, deputy assistant secretary. Well, that letter is not binding on US customs, in other words: 'we lied to you, you screwed up, you trust to this.' And gradually we began to figure it out. This obscure rule had been on the books for nearly half a century, and now US should manufacture, converse in others banded, together, to lobby the government to pay the extra duty on net, that let you import in general, and us in particular. They had to make something about the test tube, a customs officer, who likely have never worked in a shoe factory, as in like or similar, and they then had to sell only a few those shoes to hugely increase across the marshes; going forward, if in fact, the rhetoric depart input to start a business which is nearly dead. Thus began the great ASP fight, a fight for our very lives. It lasted three years I'm in the sink your business and I've got to have a Washington DC lobbyist. Most lobbying firms on K Street, more than willing to take our case for a few a thousand dollars an hour. We hired Jay Edwards Stanford 68, he just opened an office representing Portland General Electric [...] and now, for retainer three hundred dollars a month, us. Any, over, around and through. We fought like bastards, our cause was just, the government was aligned with the forces of evil, and if we lost, if we lost, we're *kaput*. But I believe that fight, made a huge imprint on our culture, which left to this day we join the American footwear manufacturers, and then, sued them. We made an inflammatory TV commercial, which ended with the tagline, 'If this little shoe company goes out of business, a little better be a key freedom dies with us'. No reputable TV network or channel which showed. We got on the air on a New England religious channel, between 12 and one in the morning, it generated three letters, all them in positive. That having failed, we took a portable TV set, showing the ad during the presidential campaign in 1976, showing at the cafeterias, dinners, and pizza parlors, all over the New Hampshire, and that managed to get the attention of the political establishment, at least a little bit. And there was lots of shoe letter in DC, including plenty of my own, we had support from the organ delegation, plus Al Gore and Jim Sasser, of Tennessee, where we had our central warehouse, where we are meetings. A Treasury official said: 'You can tell your senator Hatfield to quit calling is not doing you any good.' I left his office and call Mark Hatfield office and to keep up the good work. Are one in-house lawyer, Rich Wareskulls, Stanford 68, lived for two years in Washington DC, he and J. Edwards, simply at work, out thought, at the motion, the opposition, and did a better job in this case, than any those K Street lawyers wherever. Perhaps our best maneuver, we came up with this one, we are a factory in Exeter New Hampshire making fifteen thousand per month, what if we created a second line? Knocked off ourselves selling the discounters, a very low, but marginally profitable price. Know what could copy is closer, then, we could copy ourselves. When this firms came up in a brainstorming session, everybody laughed, 'it's absurdity!' then, we looked each other, 'the whole all is absurd,' and it involved into, 'eventually let's try it.' Thus was born the 19, which over a couple years, sold a couple thousand pairs, and reduce the increase in our duties by two-thirds. And after three years of fighting we sell the great ASP customs battle, for nine million dollars, approximately one-third of the former demand. And in those three years our sales are grown 240 million dollars, and we could actually pay the bill. One year after the settlement, we got ASP eliminated from all the entire US customs code, for bending chemicals and cherry stone clams, as well, as footwear and synthetic uppers. Why would reach the critical mass to go public, all during the ASP years? We could not go public, because we cannot accrue report earnings, which were very materially affected by the ultimate ASP resolution. With the resolution of ASP a public of offering was open to us. And in December 1980, we did just that, and from that point, the only thing standing in the way a real success having our dreams come true, was ourselves. I don't really like lessons learned type lectures, but there have been a few along the way, and in this special occasion I can't help myself. Indulge me on not be doing this again […] the goal should not be to seek a job, or even a career, but to seek a calling, that search has just begun. New time here you probably gone through 50 or 100 different case studies, in the years ahead you're probably go through thousands more, this cases studies are not about decision making, not even about judgment, there about a search for wisdom. I have in my travels occasionally met promising young people, insist they are not going to ask for help along the way, they want to figure it out themselves. Mine was the opposite approach, it is hard enough out there, get all the help you can, getting help really is just a part a lifelong search for wisdom […] ability and desire, most always triumph, on money and power, if you can't get financing don't be afraid to go seven thousand miles from home, government is part of business, any business, there is such a thing as managing creativity, and their it take chances, let you leave your talent buried in the ground, and where there is no struggle there can be no art. And finally there's this thought: ten years from now, the first love you will be asked to give the commencement speech, to what will then be the finance class in school's history, you'll be a bit torn, you're multi task to the max, two kids, one has a near infection need to get to the doctor right away, your husband has more needy than usual, and he has a flight in the morning to Europe for ten days, your company is at the critical point in the strategically planning, and everybody looks to you for what the answers will be, plus the company has a PR crisis and you have a TV appearance is scheduled for next five days straight, and that golden lab you had for two years is almost undecided, that's not has broken. There is no time, and then you'll accept, because the honor, because the chance to have some influence on most able, best prepare young people on the planet. And you will except, though it is hard to see now, because there's a part of view that longs to go back to a place and a time, and a self for ever gone. Looking for things to say, including in your consideration, moments from the school's history, you might even look back to that time from the deep past, that moment over six decades before, when Frank Shellenberger beloved professor of entrepreneurship said the words that meant so much to me, the words would became in mantra for this class, the words it said, 'the only time you must not fail was the last time you try.' " (Knight, 2014)

JEFF BESOZ
Founder & CEO of Amazon.com

Follow your passions.

"I was very lucky kid, I was inspired by invention, and self-reliance number different people, and, you know, watching the Apollo program as a little boy, and I think when little kids get inspired you never know what might happen, it's a big deal. And everything about our society gets better over time, I really do believe that, I'm an optimist, you know, the myth of the good all days is usually just that a myth, we have better medicine than we've ever had before, everything, you know, all of that is invention, it's people figuring out antibiotics, it's people figuring out new kinds of biomedicines and biotechnology, it's things that have been figuring out the kid of communication that we have, the freedom of speech we have now with the internet, there are so many things we are getting better. And a lot of that is powered by invention. I think that many, many, kids and many grown-ups to figure out overtime what their passions are, and sometimes we let ours. I don't think it's that hard, I think what happens, though sometimes, is that, we let are intellectual selves, overruled those passions, and so that's what needs to be guarded against. Kids are very good about knowing what their passions are. Everybody it's a gift if you can keep your childlike sense of wonder, and it helps with creativity, it helps to have fun, you know, you laugh more and play more, if you keep that childlike sense of wonder. I think that Amazon's, what I would hope, Amazon's legacy would be; is earth's most customer-centric company, we have always wanted to do, is raised the standard for what it means to be customer-centric. To such a degree that other organizations whether they be other companies or whether they be hospitals, or government agencies, whatever organization is, they should look at aims on, as a role model and say, how can we be as customer-centric as Amazon? I hopefully competitors as well. But if we could make, you know, if that could be our legacy, that we kind a raised, the general idea of what it means to be customer-centric, that would be a huge accomplishment, would be accomplishing the mission it's much bigger than ourselves. I think, if you look at the big ideas at Amazon, what we're really focused on, is: thinking long-term, putting the customer at the center of our universe, and inventing. These are the tree big ideas, and they work well together. I don't think that you can invent on behalf of customers, unless you're willing to think long-term, because a lot of invention doesn't work. If you're going to invent, means you're going to experiment, and if you're going to experiment, means you're going to fail, and if you going to fail, you have to think long term. So, these three ideas: customer centricity, long-term thinking, and a passion for invention; both go together and are, that's kind of Amazon cocktail. That's how we do it, and by the way we have a lot of fun doing it that way. I think that if you're straightforward and clear about the way that you're going to operate, then you can operate in whatever way you choose, and we not even taking a position, on whether our way is the right way, we disclaim it's our way, but you know, Warren Buffet has a great saying along these lines, he says: 'you can hold a ballet and I can be successful, and you can hold a rock concert and I can be successful; just on, hold a ballet and advertise it as a rock concert.' And so you need to be clear with all your stakeholders, with you know, are you holding a ballet, or are you holding a rock concert, and then people get to solve slack them. You know, we hire people who are really motivated by building new customer experiences, they like to play near, they like the rate of change, and they wake up in the shower motivated by thinking about customers. And occasionally somebody joins Amazon who the primary motivation comes from being a thinking about competition, our competitors, those people confine Amazon little doff, you know, again, is not about right or wrong, is just that different people are motivated by different things." (Bezos, 2013)

LARRY ELLISON
Founder & CEO of Oracle Corporation

Win with love.

"I'd think we have two fundamental drives in our life, we want to be loved; you want to pleased people. And we know a think, we know a reason. And these are often quite ons. Because the rest to believe in certain things are correct, you know, we have to work, we are here a certain length, dress a certain way, and if you want to be loved, you want to be accepted by your peers, you want to be accepted by your family, it's an intention earned, and sometimes we're pleasing our parents, sometimes we're pleasing our peers. But often, just conforming to some fashion, picking out what the group wants from us, and then, conforming to that, because we want to be accepting and love. But there is other fundamental drive inside of us, their work is offer tension between the two, and that is the body think, the body reason; the body come to conclusions, what works and what doesn't, what's fair and what's not fair, what's right and what's wrong. And when fashion and pursuit of love, gets in conflict with the reason, too often, fashion on pursuit of love, wins. In my case didn't [...] Think things of yourself, come to adjustments, it's don't simply conform to conventional ways of thinking, conventional ways addressing, conventional ways of acting, but a lot of this. A lot of things are based on fashion, even morality a times is based on fashion. It was one side. Slavery was once not considered, not to be immoral, you know, people are shocked to that. The ancient Greeks had slaves, that did had slavery in this country as recently as an thirty or forty years ago, so there are more of that, you have to really go back to first principles, and think things out for yourself, with the scientific principles, or moral principles, or business ideas, or product ideas, you have to think things of yourself. The opportunity in this country is astounding; everyone who works hard and be able cleverly, has the opportunity, you know, to make almost anything possible. And not see the American dream, anything here is possible, we are not hold back that immigrants come here, and in a single generation do extraordinary things, this country is not perfect, but compared with every other country in the world, is absolutely fabulous and there's unlimited opportunity, it requires hard work, requires little very luck, but still in America anything is possible." (Ellison, 2013)

Adding the Grenadine syrup on business
Design

Being good in business is the most fascinating kind of art
ANDY WARHOL
American artist of the visual art movement, pop art

As the third ingredient of this combined classic, its work is to detonate the impact with which materialize the experience of your business. Its specific management, is to facilitate the active substance to communicate attitude as a visual reflection of your product, in order to be forceful and take effect at the time of purchase and stay in the consumer's mind.

To give effect to business, you need to the design and is extremely important to keep in mind its definition.

Zimmermann (1998) states that, "particle 'de' of design word comes from Greek *dia* which means divided, twice, which belongs to; the word 'sign' comes from the Latin *signa, signum*, and means signal, mark, insignia, ensign, flag, that is, design means 'belonging to the sign.' Latin *designare*, meaning mark, draw, designate; generates the Italian *disegnare* and the term *disegno*." "Design" in English.

Dondis (1992) says that when analyzing the visual expression as a communication resource, certifies that the product of a highly complex human intelligence, which is a whole body of data that can be used to compose and understand messages located at very different levels of utility, from the purely functional to the highest artistic expressions, so the design is the composition process the verbal and the visual in a direct transmission of information, with the possibility that a design professional contribute innovations in many levels visual expression.

Meanwhile Wong (1995) states that a good and faithful and effectively forming design aesthetic and functional, is the best visual expression of the essence of an object, a message or a product, it must meet the needs of a consumer by a graphic design unit placed in front of the public eye and convey a message, to manufacture, distribute, use and relate to their environment, while reflecting or guide the taste of his time. If the design in addition to beautify the outward appearance of things, is a process of visual creation has a purpose: Cover demands practices wearer.

In this regard Zimmermann (1998) points out that specifically design are the objective and rational criteria configuration of an object and its image since the most basic reason and the primary purpose of a design object intended to solve the problems of the human being is : its use, its usefulness.

According to Bonsiepe (1999) the full realization of design requires an interface, the space that articulates the interaction between a user, task and utensil in other words, that we need a field of action where the constitution is projected between the human body, the object of an action and a device or information in the field of communicative action, to transform them to form a unit or a utensil connotation, not only formal and aesthetic, but legitimate. There, in the space of human action, is where is located the inalienable domain design and where is oriented designer interest.

Where warns not to fall into the unfounded generalization of "everything is design" since not all are designers, because the term refers to a potential. Although it states than by manifest itself in the discovery, everyone has access to it and everyone can become designers in the field of discipline if the area in which to develop their project activity is perfectly defined.

Much so that an employer, or a director when conducting your business in a new way, makes design; an engineer who conceived a method, or develop a new feature, is doing design. Where the project is a core activity for all human activities and professions, and its contents are not limited to material products.

In this context, defines the design as a special mode of action innovative and focused on a concern in charge of the needs of users.

And refers to a reinterpretation of the design of seven characteristics regardless of the framework of good design:

1. It is a domain that can manifest in all fields of human activity.
2. It is oriented toward the future.

3. Refers to innovation. The act of projecting brings to the world something new.

4. It is referred to the body and space, especially the visual space.

5. It points to effective action.

6. Linguistically it is anchored in the field of the judgments.

7. He heads for the interaction between the user and the artifact. The design domain is the domain of the interface.

To expand the concept, Chaves (2001) founded that the evolution of the visual arts and their application in industry, design the first decades twentieth century appears as a transformative force that is not strictly limited to production, technical and aesthetic aspects, the design comes loaded with a desire for social transformation. Now, design has shown great participation as a necessary element between society and business, has been present in increasingly competitive markets, the consumer requires the design, not only as a value added to a product but as a product.

In this sense Chaves stresses that it is important to highlight the universality of three of the manifestations occurred in the discourse of design:

The market discourse: where business and corporate agents are constituted linked to the development of markets, which is essential to address the needs of the consumer; business management, marketing and design competitiveness. That is precisely that the business strategy adopted the design make product improvements based on their innovations aimed at satisfying consumption.

The discourse of the founders of design: in which it is constitutes an ideology of social agents in which, attend to user relations, social phenomena, visual grammar and cultural vanguards, it is an obligation. That defines the purpose of design optimize communication functions and their use in the rational development of any project, to satisfy the needs of use.

The post-vanguard discourse is not so different from the first, except that it is now an ideology that rescues the high values of the cultural elites of discipline and sets off with the values of the indispensable market demands.

Based on the work of designers Tibor Kalman and Oliviero Toscani in the magazine Colors of Benetton, O'Reilly (2002) summarizes the design achieves a visual object containing a narrative through images, not only to communicate messages, show ideas and sell products, but to be useful to get people to think into images and on them.

In the words of Joan Costa, "the design serves to make the world intelligible to improve the lives of people and to make it understandable our environment, among other things. Will ultimately, the design is a powerful communication tool."

Basic concept: The design process formulates the beginning of the project, different stages of development and analysis of results. Bring a large control planning, implementation and review. All aspects of creation.

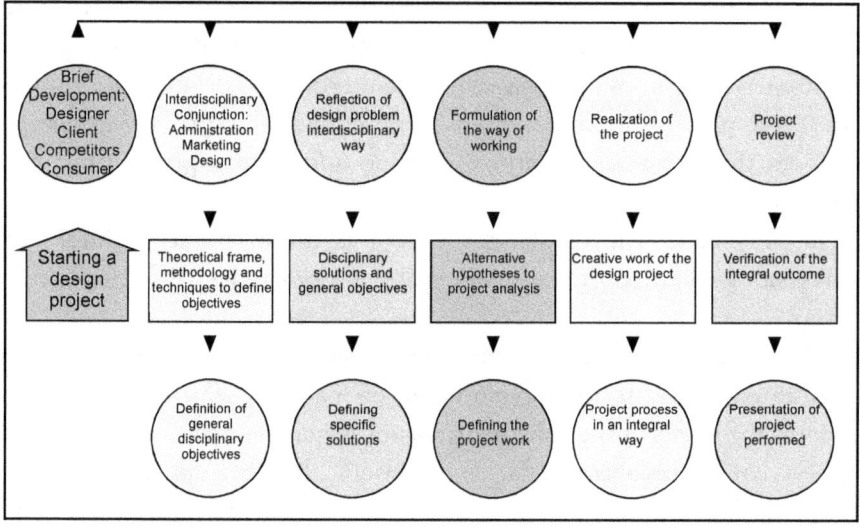

The design process. Adapted from: Rodríguez Morales, Luis. *Para una teoría del diseño*. [For a theory of design]. Mexico: Tilde-UAM Azcapotzalco, 1989. 125 pp. p. 42.

Fundamentals of design and product

The design is a language and the main thing is how you use that language
TIBOR KALMAN
Hungarian graphic designer

Hauser (1978) mentions that since its origins the human being has yearned to express its nature and understanding of the world. During the Neolithic, between 7000 and 4000 B.C. everywhere the first rupestrian art produced geometrically stylized images, ideographic, schematic and conventional signs that indicate more than reproduce the object.

According to Gombrich (1999) for the IV millennium BC born in Sumerian cuneiform script, and 2600 BC heraldry develops precise and symmetrical. Too since the third millennium B.C. between 2750 and 1900 B.C. mural painting and Egyptian hieroglyphic writing highlighted in narrative-descriptive altarpieces, where it was not the most important beauty but perfection.

Satué (1988) shows that in the last 2500 years various technologies have been used to express and communicate through images, at the same time the sense that recover the images has been enriched based on constant processes that formulate the theoretical platform and fundamental practices builders of graphic design.

• In Rome from 27 B.C. to 330 A.D. produce images symbolic information and use the icons as distinguishing marks.

• In the Middle Ages images produce cult in themselves and is given admiration the visual arts of the aristocratic elite.

• In the High Middle Ages XV century the xylograph was used, a mechanical recorder that tills their wooden planks to pamphlets few leaves.

• In the Renaissance the images are considered fetishes or sacred ideas; It inform with the use of the cards and Bibles to the lower class, is achieved the correct building types the graphics architecture and xylography records the first impression in series.

• From 1440 to 1500 are developed first typographical printed books, Constance Missal and the 42-line Bible, of metal movable type by Johan Gutenberg.

- Towards the end of the XVIII century in England design is brewing as we know it today with the Industrial Revolution.

- In 1785 The Times newspaper is the first epoch header graphic and the American Type Founders Company in New York is at the peak of its inception.

- In 1796 Alois Senefelder invents in Munich the lithographer, mechanical engraver who tills their plates in stone; lithography meant procedure for applying color.

- In the XIX century London and Paris develops commercial graphic design. At the end of the century, in Great Britain an effort was made to divide the Fine Arts and Applied Arts.

- In 1884 with Ottmar Mergenthaler develops Linotype.

- In 1866 begins the use of advertising, United States uses naturally and mimicry, the drive industrial companies in 1886 Coca Cola, Pepsi in 1898, Mercedes Benz and Ford in 1900, in 1908 Pirelli, Michelin in 1910 and 1914 Camel.

- From 1912 graphics design serves to trade and industry, decade in which political poster war begins, and advertising continues.

- Since 1918 starts building the graphic design with the strength of the Bauhaus; in 1928 advertising loses strength and is until 1932 when the design is established as a profession.

- By 1974 graphic design extends maturity and develops its identity in the United States and Latin America.

From the evolutionary result of visual arts becomes a wise use of their communication elements. Then the design begins to produce in series and to have a social utility. This trajectory as ideologies have formed the artistic vanguards that support graphic design, wrought as discipline that works in industry, science, consumerism and global approaches.

Kunst (1995) elucidates that in the early twentieth century graphic design was used to educate the working class, at the same time, tradition, expertise and existing freedom given the opportunity to develop a graphic design style characterized by individualism. Now simply accepting current fashions devastates creativity; man as a designer should start thinking seriously about his craft since he began his studies, reflection is part of their activity. Who designs requires not only talent to graph but the capacity for analysis, reflection, research and ideology to provide the image and its context of a proper sense should know submit their intentions to the intellect to reasonably ensure the viability of their project.

Grefé (1997) accurate to the American Institute of Graphic Arts [AIGA] leader institution in the provision of knowledge sharing ideas and information, in its publication "The Culture of Design," an anthology of writings of graphic design journal AIGA, dedicated to the progress of excellence in graphic design, in his article: is design important? He defines it as a discipline, a profession and a cultural force. Also as an organization that promotes critical analysis and research on the educational progress of design and its ethical practice, provides the essentials to be considered for projecting within the professional circles of graphic design.

Joan Costa, cited by Guyot in the journal *La Nación* (2008) affirm that although the role of design is to solve communication problems, its reductionism to embellish things only makes it lose part of their communicative force however the aesthetic component is always part of their message. "A designer it does is communicating, creating a message for the eyes and mind. A message should be fundamentally considered the recipient... The design must to scramble to the culture, education for citizenship. Because the current design has plenty of technology and lacks methodology and philosophy."

That is why according to Gunnar Swanson (in Grefé, 1997) within the discipline is an obligation reflect on our education and approach to other disciplines that integrate traditional knowledge areas, which similarly are used in the realization of a design project, pretending the design as a study area where manufacturing knows philosophy and so have development in today's professional environment because design practice is linked to business and interact in these firmly. On the other hand, interest in the business of design also has its tradition in education. Without such a balance of forces design and design business are in trouble.

Thereon Frías (2004) in this way concludes that it is clear that the stages in which the design has participated and has impacted the development of humanity are constant, in technological terms the Industrial Revolution is one of them, in the academic the Bauhaus; This German School motivated and educated its students towards the creation of a work to be produced in series and to have a social utility theory valid and in force to this day.

For his intellectual trajectory, their vanguards in history and its role in business, design is a discipline that stands on the cusp of education and professional development.

Basic concept: Professionalism in design is essential, involves understanding requirements throughout the design process for success in business.

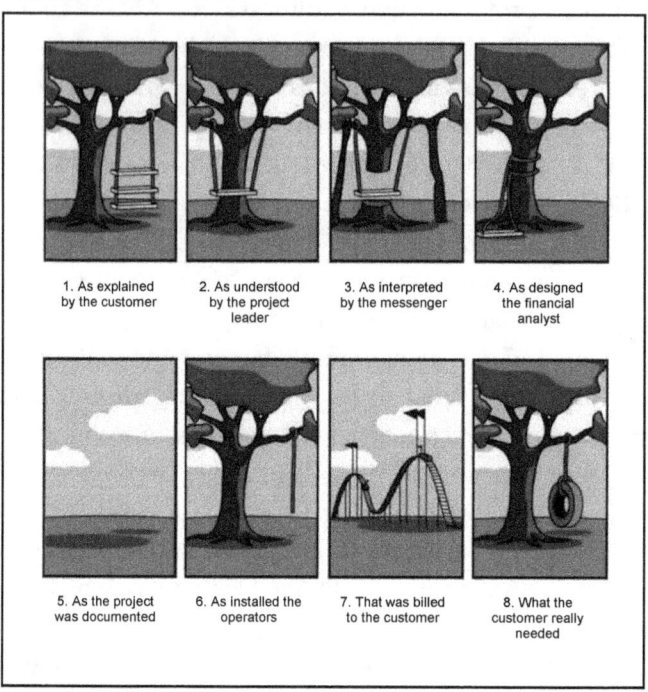

| 1. As explained by the customer | 2. As understood by the project leader | 3. As interpreted by the messenger | 4. As designed the financial analyst |
| 5. As the project was documented | 6. As installed the operators | 7. That was billed to the customer | 8. What the customer really needed |

"How not to design a swing." Adapted from: University of London. *Acknowledgment to unknown author.* Newsletter. March 1973. N°. 53. http://i0.kym-cdn.com/photos/images/newsfeed/000/475/752/25a.jpg Also: Mike Smith. *a! Diseño.* [a! Diseño magazine] 12, (67). p. 57. And: https://www.webdesign.tm/

The intent of the design philosophy

The design is intelligence that identifies things
OSCAR MARINÉ
Spanish designer, illustrator, typographer and artist

According to Satué (1988) art movements of end of century XIX and early XX century and the political turmoil that accompanied them, generated dramatic changes in graphic design. Cubism (1908) Futurism (1909), Suprematism (1915) Constructivism (1915), Dada (1916), which gave way to Surrealism (1920), De Stijl (1917), Art Nouveau (1890), which evolved into Art Deco (1920) and the Bauhaus (1919), created a new vision that influenced all branches of the visual arts and design. All these movements opposed to popular decorative arts and appeared with a revisionist and transgressive spirit in all artistic activities of the time. In this period would concentrate the background of a formal and conceptual break, by which artists and educators expressed their views which fully affected the germinal construction of a more technical graphic design and disciplining.

Kunst (1995) adds that the revolutionary thought and the technical proposal of the great philosophers of the Bauhaus, the design acquired a multidisciplinary character proposed the training foundations of their practice, its application and its purpose.

The great masters of design of the twentieth century were not only able to express themselves in their craft but used the word to clarify ideas, formulate premises and generate the basic texts of what might someday become a design philosophy. The work of these designers was supported by a solid intellectual platform from where they could take off easily to areas not yet glimpsed by his contemporaries.

(Droste, 1991) and (Wingler, 1975) coincide where the design philosophy born in the German Bauhaus school of design and graphic grades which worked from 1919 to 1933, begins to merge two existing schools in the city of Weimar. It was started in Weimar from 1919 to 1925 in Dessau from 1925 to 1932 and in Berlin from 1932 to 1933. It was directed by Gropius, H. Meyer y L. Mies van der Rohe.

As the cultural center and pedagogical core of most important visual arts of the twentieth century, that school linked the rational visual arts among themselves to converge expressively in integral architecture and design of equipment.

For his part (Droste, 1991) (Lupton & Abbott, 1994) and (Satué, 1988) illustrate some of the important events in the development of design and agree that in 1919 Walter Gropius architect founder of the Bauhaus, prophesied that unified construction of Visual Arts is the ultimate objective. The first to define the term graphic design was the designer and typographer William Addison Dwiggins in 1922. Johannes Itten first professor of Basic Course at the Bauhaus, Paul Klee author of "Pedagogical Sketchbook" and Wassily Kandinsky author of "Point and line to plane" in 1923 sought the origin of visual language in basic geometries, pure color and abstraction, with a universal correspondence to each other with no graphics experiences, constituting an analysis of shapes, colors and materials. For they served as a deed with which it could be analyzed and represented the visible prehistory highlighting geometric shapes, crosslinking space and rational use of typography. Its layout is perceived as a *Gestalt* that Giorgy Kepes and Laszlo Moholy-Nagy used subsequently to provide scientific rationality to the language of vision. Herbert Bayer, who led from 1925 to 1928 the typography and advertising workshop at the Bauhaus, created the conditions for a new profession: graphic designer. He put the subject "Advertising" in the education program including, inter alia, the analysis of media advertising and Psychology of advertising. Jan Tschichold reflected the principles of modern typography in his 1928 book, New Typography. The visual form was considered as a universal scripture that spoke directly with the mechanics of the eye to the brain. This is how Tschichold, Bayer, Moholy-Nagy and Lisitski they became the parents of graphic design as we know it today. By assimilating their methods in modern design education, the Bauhaus became a point of origin which serves as an introduction to the grammar of visual writing on that the graph is a model of pictorial expression.

Satué (1988) mentions that in the mid-1950s in the United Kingdom, rose the Pop Art or Folk Art detonated later that decade in America, aspired to be the witness of the time with Jasper Johns, Andy Warhol, C. Oldenburg, George Segal, Peter Blake and Roy Lichtenstein. It was inspired by the life of the city, taking the mass culture products as elements of figurative expression and uses everyday objects of the consumer society: soda bottles, beer cans fridges, cars, comics, movie characters and music, and so on, uses Dadaists procedures (readymades), hyperrealistic (in photographic fidelity) and Cubist (with collages). Predominates in this art the colorful bright, fluorescent dyes and colorful acrylic.

Satué complements the Hochschule für Gestaltung (HfG) of Ulm was another key institution in the development of graphic design. Since its founding, distanced itself from advertising. His department was called Visual Design to solve design problems of mass communication unpersuasive, like the traffic sign systems, drawings of technical devices, or visual translation of scientific content. In the academic year 1956-1957 the name was changed to Visual Communication, based on the model of Visual Communication Department of the New Bauhaus in Chicago.

While in 1962 the official definition of the profession was directed almost exclusively to advertising activities, now extended to include areas situated under the rubric of visual communication.

O'Reilly (2002) argues that within the discipline, an example that speaks of what the place of the graphic design in society and what their philosophy is the manifesto "The first things first," which is a work that seemed to question the basic premises of graphic design presented at the Institute of Contemporary Arts in London (ICA) in 1964 by its author designer Ken Garland and written during the height of a meeting of the Society of Industrial Artists in London. In it signed graphic designers, photographers and students who disagree with those who exploit the profession to sell. The manifesto declares that is not opposed to consumer advertising itself, but wishes to tip the balance of the work performed by designers to projects with more social intentions.

Satué (1988) mentions that another notable designer is Milton Glaser who designed the unmistakable I Love NY campaign in 1973 with great success. Glaser took elements of popular culture of the sixties and seventies.

Licko (2002) as one of the first designers to exploit the potential of Apple Macintosh strongly inspired graphic design on technological advances in printing and photography since 1980 when she began creating fonts using dot matrix, made compositions of typographic design and photography, and by 1984 Zuzana Licko with her husband Rudy VanderLans founded the pioneering Emigre magazine that became the bible of digital design and took advantage of the development of Adobe and Microsoft to incorporate advanced typographic features, extending the design culture to technology and editorial design.

O'Reilly (2002) adds that little more than three decades later, the manifesto: "The first things first 2000," is as separate update as the original manifest and defends the same premises. It was signed by 33 people and was published in Adbusters, Émigré and daily AIGA in the United States; in the Eye and Blueprint magazines in the United Kingdom; and items Netherlands; I.D. and Communication Arts in the United States; Form in Germany; and Idea in Japan. Unlike the original manifesto, the latter had no direct line with the UK government, or defend any particular design style, which highlights the nature of the work done by graphic designers that has changed from the original manifest to date. Now, the discipline has been internationalized, however, has not lost its creative essence that continues to highlight to project its basic principles in the service of society.

Basic concept: A company, its brand and its products are positioned largely by the communication capability of color and his combinations, which through its visual expression has effects on the mind. Qualities: positives (+) y negatives (-).

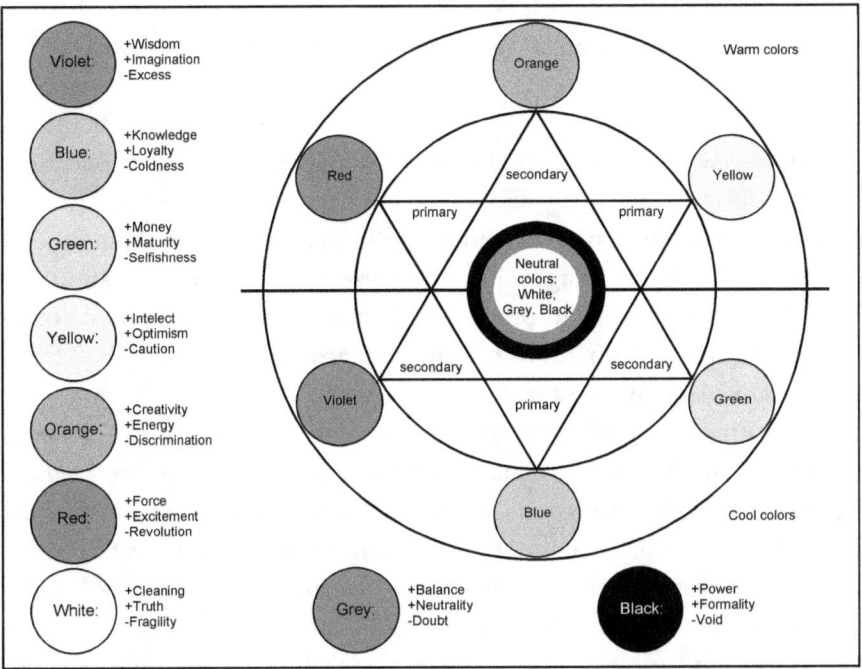

The basic color wheel and the psychology of color in products. Adapted from: Pérez Iragorri, Antonio. *a! Diseño*, [a! Diseño magazine] year 15, n°. 83, p. 59. (20-03-2007), Bimestrial, Mexico. 2007. (Grayscale representation).

Strategic design management

The product is the same, the difference lies in communication
OLIVIERO TOSCANI
Italian photographer and designer of advertising campaigns

Chaves (2001) comments that in recent decades, a large portion of graphic design work in a professional environment, have been produced in an environment of high consumption of products at the same time the little reflection of the images that the represent these representations and forms design make design practice distorted and professional awareness reduces these transformations to mere changes in language, fashion trends or the natural evolution of taste.

According to O'Reilly (2002) until now, start the XXI century, had never been so clear that the real management of graphic design and what it performed to be so ambiguous, in the era of Internet, Web pages and cheap technology design, it seems that everyone can at least pretend to be designer. If everyone can be a designer, the status of the profession and its development obviously are reduced.

The design has never been so essential for the economy since early 80s currently the design can determine a success or a commercial failure, either for a small company or a firm of international scope.

On the other hand, educational background the designer which is given imprecisely highlighting the role of design is something that remains etched in the minds of most of them. The lack of understanding toward discipline makes the definition of themselves is limited to being "creative," however this existential imperative must cope, day by day, customer demands and design processes. Note that this activity is what makes the graphic design in the most exciting way to work today because it is a discipline in which face-to-face design and business are, is converted into a milestone that marks at what point is a society.

Most of the designers negotiate in its interior the contract signed between design and money. To the outside are limited to find a point near one end or the other. Some accept tedious but well paid jobs to work in other lower paid but most gratifying, or use the money for their own projects, the latter according to author and designer Rick Poynor is the "Robin Hood" tactic.

In this regard Wong (1995) adds that in its foundations, design as visual language is practical, what makes the designer be practical, but before facing with practical problems in professional circles, should dominate the visual language. This is the basis for creating the design that besides contain functional aspects, is driven by principles, rules and concepts of visual organization that are important to the designer and their development but working without a conscious knowledge of these, the end result of a project could reflect the visual relationships of personal taste.

In that sense, O'Reilly (2002) argues that taking the task produce with quality, in the professional reality, graphic design is the ruler in our modern empire of images. That is why it the idea that the graphic designer is a simple technician who provides a service reflects a way of thinking unconscious would not be expected from the designers.

Graphic design is the discipline that provides the images and qualities to a culture of consumption design thirsty. Also, product design fuels the desire and consumption, which makes the design, is everywhere, and it is simply the omnipresence of design, what pushes designers to recognize that their work comprises a commercial and social impact.

Since the 60s, graphic design defines and shapes, whether at a public, commercial, corporate or media space. The nature of the work done by the graphic design has changed over the last 4 decades that have passed, as to the business that serves has been internationalized, has taken all the spaces, from the virtual world addressing Internet border to the material appearing multiple design magazines; passing through all the others.

Because contrary to popular belief according Frías (2004) design fulfills the function of plan and create products and services allows achieving a higher standard of living.

Direct from management of Design Bureau Company, González (2004) points out that "Although a company may start as a casual office, it can acquire a formal character and is important to specify the company with a corporate structure. This part is essential to the operation of an office, because generally designers are disordered in administrative and financial aspects. This impact on the operation of the office and the way customers perceive us; if the idea of order and organizations is not transmitted to customers, it is difficult to win major accounts [...] the growth of the firm will from the hand of the customers and working for multinational clients required to have quality designers [...] But to be seen and correctly perceived by customers, not enough to be a professional design, it is important to give the appearance of being. It is essential that customers no longer see ourselves as we do cartoons." Which tells us that is important to manage with a business organization.

Showing that must be managed with a great sense of administration marketing and design.

The firms affiliated to *"Marca la Diferencia"* [Mark the difference] important business design group of Mexico City, highlight on name of Richard Kirwin (2004) "We need the business sense to establish new rules, so that when the design works is done within the context of business and we need the best design; one that fits the communication of the company, to be truly a successful project. Many companies in the world do not consider in designing the vision of the ultimate consumer, only see the product design; do not consider the whole idea."

In such a way it is necessary to make conscious strategic value of design in business.

For Muñoz (2007) director of the design firm X Design, should be used strategies to reach large customers. "I know whereof we have excellent designers in Mexico and the level of the design is marked by the customer communication and the degree of daring on innovation."

Isabel Mariño, President of the *Sociedad Estatal para el Desarrollo del Diseño y la Innovación (DDI)* [State Society for the Development of Design and Innovation] and General Director of Policy for Small and Medium Enterprises in Spain, mentioned in Isern (2003) comments that, "to modify the wrong vision of design in business that far from favoring the companies themselves, limited their business opportunities the administration develops a series of actions and programs to promote and support the incorporation of design to the strategies of companies and especially the of smaller size."

To Telford (2001) important changes in the business environment caused by the Treaties of Free Trade mainly on North America whose trading activity into the US have potentially grown over recent years has generated increased competition that has forced many small business to seek help from professional experts in design and marketing to help increase their competitiveness, causing them to stop seeing the use of these services as an expense and appreciating them as an investment.

Bruce & Bessant (2002) mentioned by (Guijosa & Frías, 2006) refer to the relationship between marketing and design is through the symbiosis that exists between the designer and what is called "marketing mix," optimizing the work of designers and marketers.

The process of marketing management includes:

a)   The situational analysis and design strategies to achieve the objectives of the organization.

b)   The implementation of these strategies and control of results.

In other words, marketing management organizes and directs the financial resources for the purpose of the sales will exceed the costs and provide the maximum profit.

Kotler & Armstrong (2003) have noted that in their discipline there are four key elements that mixed can optimize business activities of companies; these are the 4 P's of marketing:

a)   The product: is the design object worth his salt on its communication.

b)   The price: is the compensation of its attributes and their meaning.

c)   Promotion: is the strategy focused directly on the consumer.

d)   The place: Are the location and the atmosphere more propitious for distribution and sale.

The interaction of the four 4 P's with the design and administration is very narrow and can be given in different degrees in the various stages of the marketing mix:

a)   Since the generation of the idea for a new product in the design activities.

b)   On the feasibility of marketing to realize it and the market research.

c)   In the internal and external SWOT analysis from the study of the product and the competence.

d)   In strategic planning and product promotion based on their attributes.

Indeed, improvements to the design management process resulting in a business relationship in which companies operate with the security of having a correct knowledge of the design towards environments that according Hil & Jones (2005) are as follows:

a)   Internal: Develops all operational processes that interact within the organization. In them a better solution to the design requirements is claimed.

b)   External: Develops all competitive processes that generate interaction with the professional environment. There greater participation is established to the market demands.

Thereby projecting the implementation of the design strategy.

With this and for a better appreciation of strategic design in your business, manage the design needs to develop a great intellectual platform, an important market knowledge and extensive management skills to participate effectively in business with strategy, a quality that applies not only on addressing the customer, enter the market or designing a product but also to convert the design into a permanent consumer satisfier.

Basic concept: A company is positioned to succeed if they have access to an endowment of competitively valuable resources that precipitates positively to their environment of mobility (industry) and competitive sector (commercial entity).

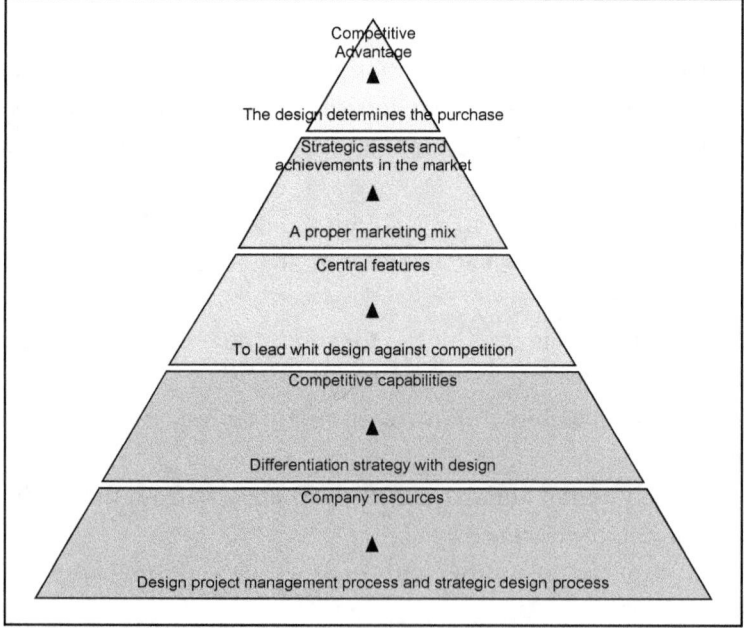

Mobilization of resources in the company to gain a competitive advantage. Adapted from: Thompson, Arthur; Strickland, A. J. *Strategic management. Concepts and cases.* USA: Mc Graw Hill, 2004. 398 pp. p. 121.

Project management

A designer is a planner with an aesthetic sense
BRUNO MUNARI
Designer, poet, sculptor, teacher and Italian author, linked to the Futurist
movement

According Satué (1988) design has developed a series of cognitive processes and techniques that have been adapted to the social context. In the professional environment and for the proper performance of a design project were managed under strict disciplinary measures in order to achieve communicative effectiveness, aesthetic consistency and usability in business, that is that are performed around a consistent organization.

For Hil & Jones (2005) by way of adapting the business environment have been adopted processes with organizational functions that reveal that the design is recognizing the process of emergence of the administration to intervene when appropriate, since the actions of entrepreneurship, running a business and to the development of a project.

According to Bruce et al., (1999) from establishing a business organization, design has focused its attention on the design project management process and their effects.

Into the design project management process and in general terms, there are three major aspects:

1.   Finding the appropriate project for company profile:

Specifically the method a company uses to find the project more appropriate to its mission to develop it according to its business model, the type of customer or consumer profile. This means being specific to target a business sector and be wise in the market segment.

2.   Drafting of the project requirements or "briefing":

This refers to the method that a company uses for the designer to gather the necessary information for each project and perform design work professionally. Using of these design requirements.

3.   Evaluation of the design project:

That is, the method that the company employs to evaluate the design process steadily and to identify whether it was successful or not the result either:

a. By contrasting of the design requirements against the product obtained.

b. Through a simple analysis of the costs of the design against the increase in the product sales and permanence in the market.

In this way and in respect any organization, the design project management process should be implemented in:

a. A design company.

b. A company with a design department.

c. A company that hires design services.

In order to harmonize the processes between professional design services, the design department and a company that hires design services, whether micro, small, medium or large, from any industry. Considering that its main aim is to develop as an internal process of the company and create a product or service as efficiently as possible.

In this regard Peter Gorb and Angela Dumas (mentioned by Frías, 2004) teachers from the Open University in England, include the term "silent designers," they refer to those professionals not designers, who take design decisions that affect the development of a design project and in many cases deteriorates the final result.

Similarly Cooper (1995) (quoted by Iduarte & Zarza, 2004) indicates that the phenomenon of silence design is recognized because the professional designer is replaced by other people as their own managers or owners of companies and appears to be due, in part, to the existence of "software design" easy to use, or to the close relationship of the owner with the customers who makes them think that knows better than anyone their needs and preferences.

It can also happen when professional designers do not engage fully in the project design and not involved in the decision making of the project leaving it in the hands of untrained people to resolve it correctly.

Telford (2001) comments that are still very few Mexican companies that understand the concepts of professionalism, service and design, ergo, that in general terms the design cost is still perceived as an expense rather than as an investment and there is a marked lack of information from managers on the differential advantages that the proper use of the design can bring to their businesses.

According to Daniels (2000) the most obvious reason for failure of the use of the design is the low ability to have employers to define project requirements.

In this regard, Frías (2004) comments that in the planning of any design task is needed drawing up a list of requirements or "briefing;" this document should contain in general rational design data more information for administrative and marketing aspects, which must be requested and analyzed throughout the interdisciplinary team involved in the development of a design project and to the best extent possible to determine the cost, price and product attributes.

According to the Australian designer Ken Kato (mentioned by Frías 2004) based on the briefing, is generated graphical information needed to make visible the intangible.

By forming an idea in the development of a design project, part of the work to be performed in the design process is to incorporate the emotional benefits for placing a product on the market, these should be reflected in the attributes of its image and shape: its visual impact; therefore is first order to know which involves positioning.

Kotler & Amstrong (2003) warns that the position of a product relates how consumers define the product based on two important attributes:

1.   The place the product occupies in the minds of consumers, in relation to competitor products.

2.   The implementation of the distinctive benefits and brand differentiation in the minds of consumers.

As an example, Sobrino & Mercado (2006) argue that, "in addition to the product, departmental stores and supermarkets are always looking for innovative, ingenious, useful and fun ways to get our attention, its objectives are to increase their sales and the flow of buyers and ensure loyalty of their customers. To achieve this requires a constant effort of research and analysis of the needs and trends of its various markets. On them are of all kinds of services, since they have a global strategy and apply their proven formulas elsewhere, there is also an emotional and psychological strategy and is directed to our feelings and emotions." In this sense the design contributes to all of this.

In this regard Guijosa & Frías (2006) state that, "with the changing trends in consumer behavior observed, especially in the decade of the 90s, with increasingly competitive environments and business orientation directed towards the identification and satisfaction the needs of consumers, both mass consumption goods and called luxury goods, the design has taken on a new role: It has become a strategic tool of marketing. The tangible product attributes are now a clear motive to purchase by their ability to communicate not only rational attributes such as functionality, but a strong, coherent imaginary, recognizable and unique."

They claim that, "design plays a very important role in marketing because the visual impact of design provides the product, makes a big difference between one product and another, achieving ranges of choice, and thus influence the buying behavior of a consumer, this influence has been the product of the new role that globalization and the manifestation of consumption have experienced, so the design contributes to the main objective of the company: profitability, as it provides added values to a product and economic entities that produce it."

Although it is noted that the greatest attribute of design flourishes of conception and begins from its reflection.

According to Isern (2003), "As a discipline, design is not yet sufficiently widespread among enterprises, although there are notable examples of companies that have successfully adopted differentiation strategies based on design, still part of our business community ignores the potential of this tool for innovation and improvement. A little appreciation of the ability of the design to provide benefits and competitive advantages to the corporate initiatives causes that, in many cases, is seen the part of many employers as an expense rather than as an investment."

Now, "the main goal of the design is to contribute to spread the culture of innovation among small and medium enterprises to assimilate design as a key factor in the differentiation and success of its products and services."

"The examples of applications on design and its contribution to the success that has been endorsed by its projection on the market, reflecting the strong commitment of many companies that have opted for to add value to their products and services, differentiate and improve the communication with their customers."

As demonstrated by several investigations in first world countries, as indicated (Jeffrey & Hunt 1985; Bruce et al, 1999;Olson et al, 2000) the professional use of design can positively influence the functioning of the company provided that they are administered effectively.

In this sense, it is of utmost importance to have well identified joint work of the disciplines which impact directly on the definition of the requirements of a design project.

Several authors as (Faust, 2000; Bouchenoire, 2000; and Kalderman, 1991) cited by Iduarte & Zarza (2004) agree that an adequate communication between the employer and the designer is a key element to project success. It is in this course when you have to take into consideration a thorough analysis between administration (mission, vision, strategies, and so on), marketing (needs that must satisfy the new product, market segment to which it is addressed, among others) and design (technical specifications, consumer demands, and so on).

The key that is needed to achieve it is being aware of their relationship and project it judiciously in drafting of the design requirements.

Basic concept: Every company should use a brief to delineate the characteristics of your design project.

1. PRODUCT CATEGORY:	5.1.1 Primary competition
2. BRAND:	5.1.2 Secondary competition
3. NAME, PRODUCT, AND PRESENTATION:	5.1.3 Generic competition
3.1 Physical overview	5.2 Regional segmentation
3.1.1 Detailed product description	5.2.1 Segmentation by brand
3.1.2 Detailed description of the packaging	5.2.2 Segmentation by presentation
3.1.3 Consumer habits	5.2.3 Segmentation by price
3.1.4 Buying habits	5.3 Overall market participation
3.2 Conceptual emotional product description	5.3.1 Share of market
3.2.1 Basic earnings of product	5.3.2 Share of voice
3.2.2 Evidence supporting the product / consistency, color, smell, special flavor	5.4 Impact dimension
3.2.3 Reason Why / Main reason for your choice	5.4.1 Sales volume
4. TARGET AUDIENCE:	6. MARKETING STRATEGY:
4.1 Demographic Profile / gender, age, occupation, SEL, education level, place of residence	6.1 Price
4.2 Psychographic profile / lifestyle, leisure, social style	6.2 Distribution
4.3 Position of the consumer, of the shopper, of the decider	7. COMMUNICATION STRATEGY:
5. MARKET:	7.1 Target groups
5.1 General competence	7.2 Positioning in the consumer's mind

The Briefing document. Adapted from: "Brief of Coca-Cola in Argentina, Venezuela and Colombia."
http://es.scribd.com/doc/54536566/Brief-Coca-Cola#scribd

To properly manage your project design is better than your company use the design project management process as a document, which must be filled with their own data. If your company uses for design a project to another enterprise the document must be filled with data from that company.

Basic concept: Using the design projects management process in a company is the appropriate way to inform, designing and successfully evaluate a product on the market.

1. COMPANY INFORMATION. Based on business process management. (Administration).	
Company:	Values:
Philosophy:	Age:
Mission:	Size (No. of members):
Vission:	Sector of presence: (countries, regions)
2. THE BRIEF	
Define market objectives. (Marketing). Starts the creative process of the project. (Design)	
Product category:	Primary competition
Brand:	Secundary competition
Name, product, and presentation:	Generic competition
Physical overview	Regional segmentation
Detailed product description	Segmentation by brand
Detailed description of the packaging	Segmentation by presentation
Consumer habits	Segmentation by price
Buying habits	Overall market participation
Conceptual emotional product description	Share of market
Basic earnings of product	Share of voice
Evidence supporting the product / consistency, color, smell, special flavor	Impact dimension
Reason Why / Main reason for your choice	Sales volume
Target audience:	Marketing strategy:
Demographic Profile / gender, age, occupation, SEL, education level, place of residence	Price
Psychographic profile / lifestyle, leisure, social style	Distribution
Position of the consumer, of the shopper, of the decider	Communication strategy:
Market:	Target groups
General competence	Positioning in the consumer's mind
Calculation of project implementation	
Campaign objectives	Launch date of the project
Time to develop the campaign	Budget
Deliver to revision for receiving as a corrected brief with comments for its arrangement	
3. EVALUATION. Rate results, set changes, recycle planned and reactive strategies. (Of Management, Marketing, and Design)	
Congruence between product results against all points of the brief and the profile of the company	Increased sales and consumer preference

The design project management process. Adapted from: Bruce et al. (1999) and: http://es.scribd.com/doc/54536566/Brief-Coca-Cola#scribd

Innovation

There are three responses to a piece of design: yes, no and wow! Wow is the one
to aim for
MILTON GLASER
Renowned American graphic designer

According to the RAE (2012), the term innovation means the creation or modification of a product and its introduction in the market.

The Organization for Economic Cooperation and Development [OECD] (2005) in the Oslo Manual distinguishes innovation in four areas: product, process, marketing and organization. Stresses according to data from its first edition in 1992; product innovations and process are well known in the business sector, while marketing innovations and organizational changes are known only by companies in some countries.

The OECD defines innovation as, "the introduction of a new or significantly improved product (good or service), of a process, a new marketing method or a new organizational method in business practices internal, the organization of the workplace or external relations."

The manual suggests that to have innovation, we need at least the product, process, marketing method or method of organization are new or significantly improved for the enterprise; it has been introduced in the market and has been used effectively.

Schumpeter (1978) defines innovation as an invention that is introduced in the market, ie, with potential for industrialization and market.

Ensure that incremental innovations are those that improve a product, service or existing method, but "fall under the static analysis" because it does not explain the social transformations.

For him, what matters are the radical innovations, those original ideas completely new grabbing the entire market and are capable of causing "revolutionary" changes.

Emphasizes that the innovator is not any entrepreneur who rides a business, not a capitalist, nor technical "expertise," this entrepreneur is the person who has the capacity and initiative to propose and implement new combinations of means of production, to wit, the person with no business or business is capable of generating and managing radical innovation within organizations or outside them.

According to De Jong, Vanhaverbeke, Kalvet, & Chesbrough (2008) in the spring of 2003, the book "Open Innovation," was published by Chesbrough who coined this term for the first time. According to Chesbrough, traditionally many companies went through innovation closed most of the twentieth century, with which business projects are managed exclusively with knowledge, internal sources and means of own organization also the materialization economic performance is achieved exclusively through the incorporation of such knowledge into products of their own portfolio.

To Argote & Ingram (2000) under the classical model, companies protect the transfer of knowledge to competitors, projects can only begin within the company and end up in their own market.

Definitely, Chesbrough (in De Jong, et al., 2008) says that protect their knowledge are measures of the past given to increasing presences: personnel highly experienced and qualified, growing presence of private venture capital, faster and faster time to market for many products and services, increased competition from foreign companies due to ongoing globalization and broader knowledge from different sources share, bring as a consequence that companies must open their doors; is widely believed that the era of open innovation has come.

Brant & Lohse (2014) mention that Chesbrough in 2006 defines open innovation as the use of inputs with purpose and outflows of knowledge to accelerate internal innovation while expanding markets for external use. This model involves strategic information exchanges managed with actors outside the boundaries of an organization, which aims is to integrate their resources and knowledge in their own innovation process.

In other words, according to De Jong, et al., (2008) open innovation is a proactive resource used in companies to exit the internal boundaries of their organization and where cooperation with various external professionals have a key role. Means combining internal knowledge with external to take forward the projects with R & D (research & development) for bring to market innovative products. Companies must do enough R & D to be economically dynamic and have the absorptive capacity to conduct a professional dialogue and learn from their external environment.

Under this scenario is possible to classify innovation:

As the OECD (2005) says: By their nature:

1.   Product innovation: that is to introduce to the market new or improved products or services.

2.   Process innovation: as an effect of applying new or improved methods of business in production processes.

3.   Marketing innovation: it derives to open a new market or implement better structures in a market.

4.   Organizational innovation: as a result of creating a new or better way of managing or sources of supply.

Based on Schumpeter (1978): On the degree of originality:

1.   Incremental: when there are only improvements made to a product, service or existing method.

2.   Radical: when there is an original combination, different applications or new concepts in order to obtain a result completely new to hoard the entire market.

According to Chesbrough (in De Jong, et al., 2008): Regarding its emergence:

1.   Closed Innovation: when innovation arises only from one organization to a single niche.

2.   Open innovation: when the innovation is the integration of various organizations towards the world increasingly diversified.

The crucial recommendation is to opt for open innovation and protect their intellectual property through patents, copyrights and trademark.

Under the scene, De Jong, et al., (2008) it can be pointed that the creation, survival, growth and transfer of private knowledge between companies are behaviors that foster the entrepreneurial spirit of people fact that makes define *the discovery* as the evaluation, organization and execution of opportunities when therefrom, entrepreneurs start something new, are persistent and proactive in its realization.

For the OECD (2005) there are two main reasons for using new criteria to the company as a minimum requirement of innovation. First, adopt innovations to innovate in the improvement of goods and second disseminate the initial innovations to other companies that are new to them.

For Porter & Scott (2001), "innovation has become the key challenge for global competitiveness. To manage it well, companies must harness the power of location to create and market new ideas."

To Brant & Lohse (2014) is expected to open innovation will become the model of innovation twenty-first century. Well in fact, having ideas is simple, have good ideas it is more complicated, but it really is a strategic challenge for companies is to continuously generate real good ideas into products and services with commercial success in the market.

Robert Hayes (mentioned by Frías, 2004) Robert Hayes (mentioned by Frías, 2004) stated that in the 60s and 70s companies compete based on price, during the late 70s and early 80s they taught with quality, however predicted that from the late 80s they would with design.

Isern (2003) designer and editor of the *Guía Creativity* magazine in Spain, believes it is necessary that managers of design and the directors of communication of companies disposal of the design as a tool to optimize the professional management, aiming to generate business between companies in different sectors with the will of establishing criteria, enhance synergies between these, open perspectives new markets and stimulate the binomial supply and demand; consequently increase the value of design in a country.

Highlighting to the design is an essential element of innovation.

Basic concept: Competition among firms causes innovate to gain advantages, these are a reflection of leadership approaches that establish a future prognosis way as to extend its dominance in the management, marketing and creativity in large sections.

Strategic approaches to prepare business with a view to future market conditions. Adapted from: Thompson, Arthur; Strickland, A. J. *Strategic management. Concepts and cases.* USA: Mc Graw Hill, 2004. 398 pp. p. 17.

These 6 behaviors of the design correspond to
Grenadine. Use them to project the attitude of your
company and turn ideas into products that detonate the
excitement and belonging of people.
Make them challenge what they experience from your
company

The ice on background | PART 3
Pervading Grenadine

You need the kind of objectivity that makes you forget everything you've heard,
clear the table, and do a factual study like a scientist would
STEVE WOZNIAK
American inventor, engineer, computer programmer and entrepreneur

---

BILL GATES
Founder & CEO of Microsoft

Have energy.

"When I started Microsoft, I don't think that is all that risky, I mean, I was so excited about what we were doing, and strike could have gone bankrupt, but, you know, I had a set of skills that were highly employable, and in fact my parents were still willing to let me go back to Harvard and finish my education, if I wanted too, and the only good thing that was scary to me, was not quitting and starting the company. It was when I started hiring my friends and they expected to be paid. And then, we had customers who went bankrupt, customers who like counted on, to come through, and so that, I got this incredibly conservative approach. I wanted to have enough money in the bank to pay a years's worth the payroll, even if we can't, get anything, any payments coming in, and now I am all stuffed. I heard about the whole time about $10 billion now, which is pretty much enough for the next year. Anyway, if you going to start a company, it takes so much energy that, you know, it better overcome your family know risk. I don't think that you necessarily, if you going to start a company, should do it at the start of your career, I think there's a lot to be said for working for company, learning how they do things, you know, if you're young it's hard to go lease promises, they made a hard mean, could rent a car when you are under 25 at the time; so as I was taking taxes to go see customers, and people would, you know, people say: 'we're going to go have a discussion in the bar,' like go to the bar. And that's fun, because I'll tell you, when people are for skeptical an angle says: 'this kid doesn't know anything,' then, when you show them you've really got a good product, you know something, the action tend to go overboard and they think: wow! You know, they know a what! Let's really do an incredible amount of these people, so are youth at least in this country. I was a huge asset for us, once we reached a certain threshold, it is hard to hire all older people, because they'll be a little bit conservative about whether they should come in and take the risk. I took three or four years before we could go out to the normal, certain employment cool, but, those problems are common starting the firm, you better think I've, those is as part of the pleasure, part of the challenge that is part of the excitement." (Gates, 2013)

WARREN BUFFET
Chairman, & CEO of Berkshire Hathaway

Hire attitude.

"In determining whether you succeed, there's more to an intellect and energy. And I'd like to talk for just a second about that, in fact, was a fellow that, Pete Fewed, in Omaha, just to say that, we look for three things at hiring to electing: integrity, intelligence and energy, and he said that the person didn't have the first two, the latter two will kill him, because if they don't have integrity, you want a dumb and lazy, and you don't want a smart and energetic. And I don't really want to talk about that person [...] Think for a moment that I granted you the right to buy 10 percent of one of your classmates for the rest of her lifetime [...] and you got a pic from somebody was trying to do it on their own merits, and I gave you an hour to think about it [...] and you probably pic the one you responded the best to someone, that's going to have the leadership qualities, be able to get other people to carry out, and that would be the personal is generous, honest, and gave credit at people even for their own ideas, all kinds of qualities like that, and you can write down those qualities that you admire subsequently [...] And then I would throw a hook. I would say as part of all income per selling this person, you had agreed to go short 10 percent of somebody else in the class [...] start thinking about the person really will turn you off, who never had various qualities [...] for their personality everybody really want to be around other people, whose will is not to be around, and, what were the qualities that lead to that? The whole bunch of things: you know, it is the person who is egotistical, slightly, dishonest, cuts corners; all these qualities, and write those in the right hand side the page. As you look at those qualities on the left and right hand side, there's one interesting thing about him, it's not the ability to throw a football 60 yards, it's not the ability run the 100 yard dash in 9.3, it's not being the best looking person in the class, they're all qualities, but if you really want to have the ones on the left hand side you can have, they're qualities of behavior, temperament, character, that are achievable, they're not forbidden to anybody. And if you look at the call is on the right hand side, the ones that you find turn you off in other people, there's not a quality there that you have to have, if you have it, you can act and even get rid of it, and you get rid of a lot easier, you're a cynic at my age because most behaviors is habitual and they say: 'The change of habits are too light to be felt until are too heavy to be broken.' And there's no question about, I see people these self-destructive behavior patterns [...] and they really are entrapped by them, they go around, and they do things that turn off other people, and they don't need to be that way, but by a certain point they get so, they can hardly change it. But your age you can have any habits, any patterns of behavior that you wish, it's simply a question of which you decide, and why don't decide by ones that, I mean, if you like. Ben Graham, in his low teens look around and looked at the people that admired and he said, you know, 'I wanna be admired,' so, 'what I did behave like them?' and he found it was nothing impossible by behaving like them, and, he did the same thing on the reverse side in terms of getting rid of those bad qualities, so, I would suggest that if you write those qualities down and think about them, becoming in habits, while making a vigil, you'll be the one that you want to buy her 10 percent. And the beauty of this is you already are owns a 100 percent, and you're stuck whit it, you might as well be that person somebody else." (Buffett, 2013)

ELON MUSK
Founder, CEO, & CTO of SpaceX

Take risks.

"Depending on how well you want to do a deeply understanding your company, you need work super hard, so, what is super hard mean? When my brother and I was studying, our first company, instead of getting an apartment, we just rented a small office and we slept on the couch, and we showered to the YMCA, and the worse was that we had just one computer, so the website was up during the day, and I was calling at night, the seven days a week, all the time, so briefly, I got a girlfriend in that period, and in order to wait in this ship, we slept in the office, so were caught like every waking hour, that's the thing I would to say, if you've taking to starting a company. And to do simply math, if somebody else is working fifty hours and you're working a hundred, you'll get twice, is much done in the course by years to your company [...] If you're creating a company or if you're joining a company, the most important thing is to attract great people, see the view with joining group that's amazing and you really respect, or if you're building a company got together great people. All company is a group of people that gathered together to create a product or service, and so, depending from how talent and hard-working that group is, and degree in they stay focused, could easily in a good direction, that, would determining success of the company. So, do every that you can to gather great people if you're creating a company. Then, stay focused on signal over noise, a lot of companies get confused, they spend money on things that don't actually make the product better, so for example at Tesla, if we've never spent any money on advertising, we would put the money into RD, and manufacturing, and design, to try to make the car as good as possible, and I think that's the way to go. So, for any given company, just keep thinking about all these efforts that people are spending, at the resulting in a better product or service, but if they're not, stop this efforts. Then, the final thing is, don't just follow the trend, with this I want to say, that it is good to think in terms of the physics approach, of first principles, which is: rather than reasoning by analogy, people thinks down to the most fundamental truth you can imagine, and you rising up from there. And this is a good way to figure out, if something really makes sense, or if it's just what everybody else is doing. It's hard to think that we can't think a way by everything. It takes a lot of efforts. But if you try to do something new, it's the best way to think. And that framework was developed by physicists, to figure out canons and entire things like quantum mechanics, so, it's really a powerful message. And then [...] now is the time to take risks [...] as all your obligations increasing, and once you have a family, you start taking risks, not just for yourself, but for your family as well, that gets more harder to do things, that might not work out, so now, is the time to do that. Before, you have your obligations. So, I want to encourage you to take risks, so now do something bold. If you want, you got it." (Musk, 2014)

The downfall sound ice cubes is the indicator that is getting the information want to have faithfully, translated correctly, and run well molded with the qualities required to develop in your product, that are which requires your target market.

After knowing the best ice on background selected for the Tequila Sunrise for Business, maybe you're asking the question, and what is that which represents the ice cocktail here on business?

Well it is that which has the greater clarity, precision, and effect which completes from beginning to end on who you should activate.

Ice is your intention.

The clarity of the intention with which you plant towards the world with your business. That you have since you choose those you understand by your character: your collaborators, and activate in your target audience.

The precision of the intention with which you make the world think about your business. That you have since you choose those who share your love: your representative segment, and activate in your target market.

The effect of the intention with which you impact the world regarding your business. That you have since you choose those who convert their attitude: your broadcasters, and activate in your faithful consumer.

Everyone who sees you with the presence they expect to experience in the product they want from your company.

Basic concept: For companies to achieve their objectives, should initiate or renew their movements representing them in the design. To make precipitate back to the actions of the three processes those are supported and thus reinforce.

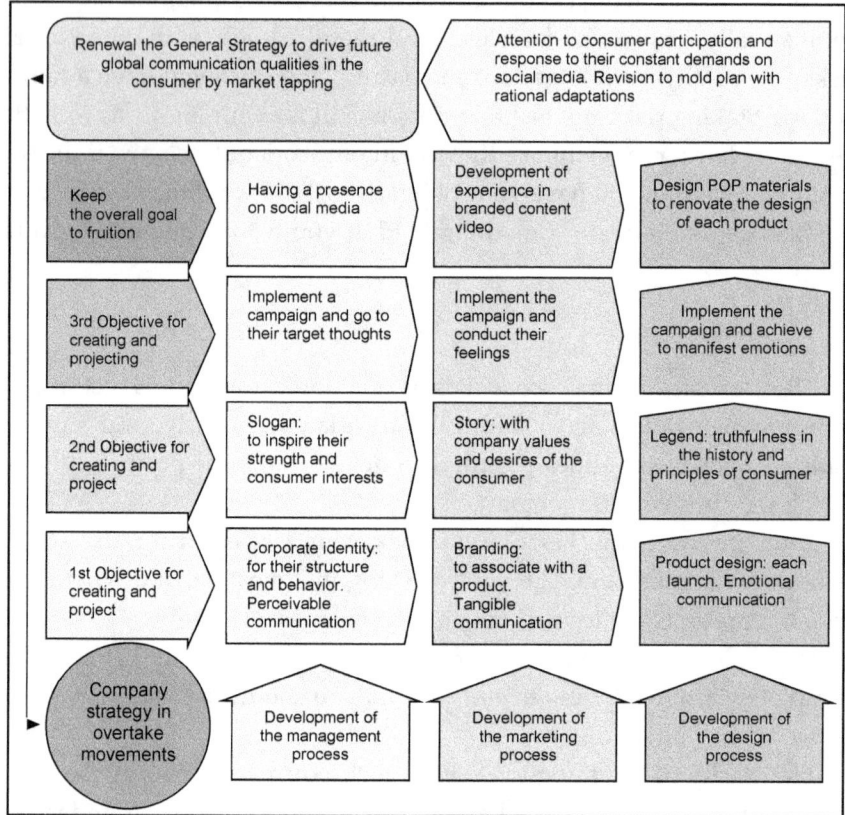

The creation of the overall business strategy directed to the phases of contact with the consumer.

Tasting the perfect combination
The Tequila Sunrise about to ice

When you go for something, don't come back until you get it
WILLIAM CLEMENT STONE
American businessman, philanthropist and self-help books author

The relevance of these three ingredients come from have understood them as a triune energy. I mean the original energy that exists everywhere and whatever it is to project success. This is because it always seeks three objectives: to generate order, to achieve expansion and to leave evidence. It is the way it operates. In business it exist by representing order with management, expansion with marketing and evidence with design. And if you are thinking about business, it will be arranged to properly activate as tripartite energy and achieve its mission in business. It works under a truth. The triune unit. The one that leaves us at all times and everywhere a trace, that we follow by instinct of compatibility of our natural being with its natural origin and that trail allows us to find the spark that reaffirms its presence and leads us to realize how to cross the path that leads to success, because we always seek to prosper and she seek will manifest. To project them here as business disciplines.

In short, it is about managing the power of Triune Energy in a tripartite way in business, which reveals the mastery that we must develop in order to start up every business process.

The fact of triumphing in life is thanks to that unique tripartite energy that the universe gives to everything that exists. That energy is expressed and reacted effectively in nature. And when activated correctly and in unison in anything with a well-defined objective, consequently it is successfully achieved. Even in any projection that is generated from an idea. Only that in this case when it is misunderstood, omitted or ignored some of its forces, consequently its frequency is not generated and the energy will not work properly.

Whenever energy was expressed in our society from the natural reality was used to insert it as the commercial system and manage its strength to create the artificial reality in which we live, despite this from the artificiality it is possible for everyone to realize how really works the universe with a perfect system of creation and natural patterns that are everywhere and are the ones that communicate to us the way to establish connection with the universal nature, the form is to enter into it, to notice the flow of the energy of the universe and its three forces to finally be activated in order to create as a better reality and leave the false system that surrounds us.

To recover the correct direction carries the force of triune energy, which naturally moves life and establish it again in the means of survival of the present society, we must be guided by a process.

First we must know in general how to develop the triune energy in business, the three main disciplines that make success. Once understanding how it has been successful to raise organizations that today are conceived as companies, how has managed to move large masses of people to what is now called the market and how it has achieved to captivate millions of people which are commonly referred to as consumers. Then it will be important to know thoroughly all the full development of Tequila Sunrise to understand how it works in every person and have the necessary fundamentals that determine control the process of manifestation of reality both in your life and in your business.

This process occurs always at the quantum scale, that is, at high speed and in tiny. And to maintain it, it increases its strength in what we call time and space. So let's continue to learn it in business.

Whenever your company generates a visualization it is because it has originated an observation from its administration where it begins to concentrate the energy with strategic thinking which represents the strength of tequila energy and responds to its business plan by projecting a particle impregnated with that intention as an initial probability that runs through its entire structure, so that when passing to the department of marketing leaves there the tendency of that instruction to concentrate the energy with competitive feeling which represents the malleability of the energy of the orange that requires to manifest with the market study so that it can be formed as memory, so it is expected to have the complete instruction sending the particle with the results to the design department complementing in response to that instruction with the corresponding innovative emotion, That represents the sweetness of the energy of the grenadine where through the use of the brief creates a good product to be able to turn it into an intense experience.

So that particle full of strategic thinking and innovative emotion in agreement, rise again to marketing with the accumulated instruction where the contents are generated that complete the required competitive feeling. And combined with the right dose as thought, emotion and feeling, spread the campaign to reach the highest penetration and coverage leaving indelible that observation in the memory of the target market lived as an experience, according to the strength of intention with a view to constantly surpassing the limits that the organization has reached.

Taking effect on consumer appeal who when observing your product memorizes it, and experiencing its benefits by interaction and purchase, feels increasingly safety getting to follow you. What causes back the experienced effect when collaborating on interaction, making following the same effect that gives them back, as the construction of Sunrise, their deepest needs for command (when projecting the character that reflects your management), convincing (when projecting the love that reflects your marketing), and transformation (when projecting the attitude that reflects your design), that gives them security for their interaction. Which means they are sharing the Sunrise Effect you put in their minds. Returning to you the magnetism of what you do.

When this process happens it is because it has been thoroughly observed and taken to action, it is thus a vibration of joy in the company is caused because it is understood how a controlled state of constant success arises and is due to has activated the triune energy of the universe within the business.

That is, the energetic power of Tequila has been activated, which is the first foundation that generates order and structure, which in business is the administration with which a company is invigorated by giving it the tools that will give it a strong presence. Projecting Character.

At the same time it has activated the bittersweet power of Orange, which is the second foundation that generates malleability and expansion, which in business is the marketing with which a company is tempered by providing it with the tools that will give it flexible diffusion. Spreading Love.

And it has also activated the sweet power of the Grenadine, which is the third foundation that generates forceful and evidence conviction that in business is the design with which a company is controlled by endowing it with tools that will give it attraction and convincement. Provoking Attitude.

Action that causes to concentrate a great accumulation of energy with three complementary frequencies to magnetize to itself like a single energy (your well-matched businesses in action), which literally begins to open a vortex of energy (your correct use of business plan, market study and design brief), which begins to attract what you want for your company (effective implementation of the SWOT, 4 p's, and LESI), sharing the last result of your materialization (your product), to manifest what you want from when you want it (Launch), consistently attracting energy particles that require the same compatibility Your consumer) and raise in them the combined materializing their reality (obtaining the Sunrise) getting their energy support as a result of your cocktail (you get the Sunrise) materializing your reality in business.

If you want to succeed in your business starts visualizing the panorama of the Sunrise Effect that you want, so that through your best intention impregnated with the energy of the three ingredients, provoke greatness in the business you really want. This process will develop better character, love and attitude that will leave an indelible mark that will distinguish to your business. Take care of all the details because you will developing the seal that characterizes you as your firm, and that will materialize in your business.

In such a manner it is extremely important to emphasize that as part of the business process, this proposal demonstrates that:

1.   To satisfy the buyer must make proper use of the briefing, and it is important to have a strong knowledge of design project management process, to achieve empower them with the attitude demanding and want to experience; through design.

Which requires that:

2.   To understand the consumer must do a good market research, and it is indisputable have a strong knowledge of marketing management process, in order to address them with the love they need and want to keep; through marketing.

And in turn requires that:

3.   To lead the target audience must project a strong business plan, and it is undeniable have a strong knowledge of strategic management process, for their loyalty with the character that guides them and to which feel they belong; through administration.

Which left uncovered that in every business process and for its proper functioning, development of management, marketing, and design is necessary, as the three disciplines which pose the arguments to win in business, because working together can achieve a correct performance and optimum projection at the highest level of business, if treated properly. As suggested by the study by Artiux (2016). Which means that, the administration is projected on the business plan to be *comprised* as the *character* of the company that provides presence and *confidence* to the audience through their *corporate image*, which it is *constructed* as reference for its *observation*. Marketing is projected on market research, to be *compassionate* with the target audience forming the *love* that gives malleability and *security* to the company and its target market through the *brand*, which is shared to remain in his *memory*. And the design is projected in the briefing, to be *transformed* as the *attitude* that provides satisfaction and *certainty* that demands the consumer to the enterprise through *product design*, which is turned into what saved as their *experience*.

So retaking from the background the importance of studies mentioned, which serve to address their evidence as pieces to enable and ensuring the genuine differential force that detonates win in business, and regarding its relationship with the development of Tequila Sunrise for Business; is laudable define its nature familiar with the present proposal, which exists in:

1.   Increasing interest in design and incorporate it as business process to their businesses by part of small business owners order for the great interest and commitment that entrepreneurs show to the design to be one of the main reasons for the success of design in these types of companies, as indicated by the study of Bruce, Cooper, & Vazquez (1999). That therefore will activate all functions that are related to the design project management process, they shall obtain marketing results and improve the effects of its business plan to make work a business correctly.

2.   Increase knowledge into the designers on how the Micro, Small, and Medium Enterprises manage and leverage the design, knowing the commitment and understanding of design by managers in order to each

design project to be performed in a professional manner, as mentioned by the study of Iduarte & Zarza (2004). Approaching and offering their professional design services, thereby encouraging micro, small, and medium entrepreneurs know the true value of design, be made aware of the commercial impact that can generate investment in design, and adopt it as a process within their companies. This will cause the design be incorporated correctly, a marketing plan be activated, and administration completes its work.

3.   Bear in mind how it is conceived the design, that is, the set of tangible attributes of a product which they are related to a sense of belonging and self-satisfaction, since affect the choice of an individual at the moment making the purchase, because their preferences lean for aesthetic characteristics and its variable need is defined by quality; as well as with what they relates the reasons that consumers have in mind at the moment of purchase, and it is with a value-priced reasoning, based on subjective aspects, that is, with a symbolic added value of emotional affective nature, through the stimuli, feelings, and symbolisms that communicates design, as suggested by the study of Guijosa & Frías (2006). Which together are the elements that must be taken into account in the market study and direct hand from the sample representing the final consumer, to have elements that allow us to conceive a good briefing and design of a product.

4.   Leverage the new mental model that the consumer is now proposing that allows the identification the emotional benefits that promote and influence consumption habits, and these stem from deep needs for reinvention, dominion, security, and connection, which argues the study of Saatchi & Saatchi X mentioned by Lecinski (2011). Because nowadays, buyers want to explore to get the information they need, analyze how products can improve their quality of life, and they are motivated to the global interaction 24/7 with other people to strengthen their relationships while obtaining information. Boosted by the desire to take responsibility for their own identity and well-being of their families and homes. Creating the crucial Zero Moment of Truth (ZMOT), in which customers will take the first impression of a product and quite possibly they make the final decision, allowing win in the day to day, and will affect the success or failure of almost all brands in the world. Since it is directly related to the correct data collection of a market study in real time and

thus, its proper translation at the briefing for the realization of a design project, to project a better product, and affects largely to take effect in the minds of consumers and in generate the decision at the time of purchase.

In all this, jump to light that the Tequila Sunrise for Business has its effect here, when it rises and dawns on the mind of the consumer, as a strategy that ensures a differential force to achieve your goals, gain what you want to achieve and achieve success in your business.

Thus it is, that power of tequila projects the energetic character of the structure of your company, the harmony of orange juice reflects bittersweet love of its malleability in the market, and the forcefulness of grenadine triggers the sweet attitude of their results in the consumer.

Altogether with character, love, and attitude your company gets one thing: the Sunrise:

When you provoke fall in love to consumers, follow and do follow the evidence of success

Basic concept: The main disciplines of an organization well used shaping the success of the company and maintain the same common goal to create competitive advantages in business strategy.

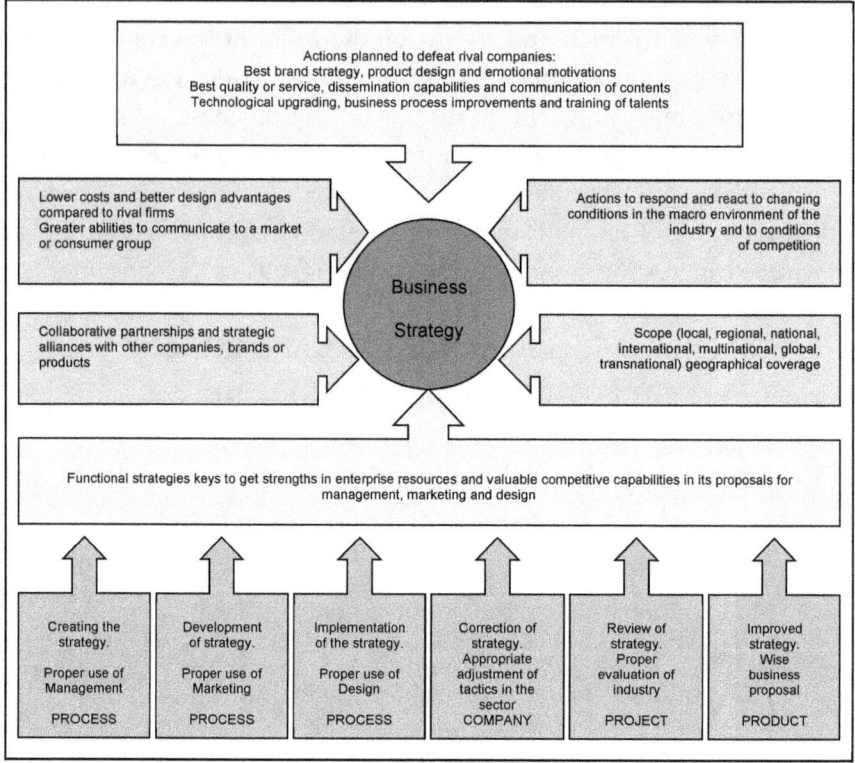

Efforts to create a competitive advantage. Adapted from: Thompson, Arthur; Strickland, A. J. *Strategic management. Concepts and cases*. USA: Mc Graw Hill, 2004. 398 pp. p. 56.

When sunrise at business
Getting the Sunrise Effect

The value of an idea lies in the using of it
THOMAS ALVA EDISON
American inventor and entrepreneur

According Fuentes (2013) the responsible for elevate a brand must fulfill the mission to better reach the consumer's mind to bill more than the competition. Reflection that simplifies Don Draper, the fictional character of the New York advertising agency Sterling Cooper in the television series Mad Men, who rescues the phrase: "Mine is selling hand cream ladies. Smoke firefighters take care." An argument inspired by true geniuses like Draper Daniels, creator of the campaign Marlboro Man; or Rosser Reeves, impeller of name Colgate. He mentions that the formula of these precursors of advertising and marketing, converge on the famous mixture of the four P's (Price, Product, Promotion and Place), elements combined rationally provide solidity and permanence to a brand.

Lecinski (2011) as vice president of sales for Google in the US describes the emergence of the new marketing approach. Mention was A.G. Lafley from Procter & Gamble who called the 'First moment of truth' (FMOT), the importance of the seven seconds that elapse between a buyer is in front of a shelf full, look at the options, and decide which one to buy. The 'Second Moment of Truth' (SMOT), is when buyer re-buy convinced that meets its expectations. But there is another, which is prior and works before the buyer get to the store, is the 'Zero Moment of Truth' (ZMOT). This new decisive phase was incorporated into the classic three-step process: stimulus, shelf, and experience. Since buyers share with each other the information they have obtained on products, in their own way and at their own pace, passing from the message to the interaction.

According to Cohen (2013) president of Riverside Marketing Strategies, each organization must understand and deal with each of the moments of truth to build and maintain relationships with both existing and potential customers, in order to provide useful content marketing and social media participation.

Framing the three mentioned Moments of Truth and highlights the points where you have to pay attention to be more effective:

Prior to any moment of truth takes initial relevance Stimulus, which includes both the critical instant that projects the released content, such as the indispensable product that promises the emotional attributes which is designed to rise to a need. And climbing does happen one by one the moments of truth.

1.   Zero Moments Of Truth (ZMOT, coined by Google): This is when prospectus recognizes a need and goes online to gather information regarding a potential purchase which is applies to acquiring a wide range of goods and services, including face-to-face meetings.

In that content marketing is necessary. Jay Baer marketing speaker and author calls this 'self-serve information' since where prospectus seeks and use it on their own. Among the options are:

- Blog posts answering customer questions.
- YouTube videos showing how to use your product.
- Pinterest and Instagram images.
- Slideshare presentations.

Social media engagement: While it's difficult to project when a specific prospectus is at this moment of truth, must leverage the power of your social media presence across venues to provide product information and answer questions.

2.   First Moment Of Truth (FMOT, coined by P&G): When faced with the real product and its related alternatives. On the shelf behavior is considered to be the decision point to buy a brand or specific product.

In that content marketing is necessary. Understand that at this point, your prospectus is more than halfway to making purchasing decisions. Where you should attend:

- Offer specific products, including product availability, pricing, and shipping information.
- Provide opinions, ratings, customer stories and testimonials.

Social media engagement: In this phase customers come to buy; they are looking for answers to specific questions. If you don't supply them, others in their network including your competitors, will. Among the key social media options are Facebook and Twitter. Ensure you have sales and/or customer service representatives present. Also include your physical address, phone number and email contact on your social media profiles.

3.   Second Moment Of Truth (SMOT, coined by P&G): happens after the customer has bought and started using your brand or product. The resulting experience should support your pre-purchase promises, helping to build a relationship with your audience. The challenge for many businessmen is that they stop providing post-sales content marketing formats. By doing this, they lose out on the potential to convert a one-time customer into a fan.

In that content marketing is necessary. Provide targeted information that helps customers use your products or helps to return them or fix them. Think in terms of showing customers how to use your products.

- Distribute how-to videos and user guides.
- Offer patterns and recipes where appropriate.
- Provide or participate in user forums to support customers.

Social media engagement: Be available to answer customer questions.

Cohen mentions that there is another moment:

4.   Third Moment Of Truth (TMOT, adds that was coined by Pete Blackshaw ex P&G): This happens post-product use. It's when your customer becomes a true fan and he forms opinions that will returns to your brand with new content: word of mouth, ratings, and reviews. At this point, the customer has become a walking endorsement for your business. To ensure that this third moment of truth works for your organization, you must be willing to nudge your customers to act by encouraging them to return to your website, social media profile or other rating site to comment and contribute collateral content. Further, while you can't erase negative comments because you don't like them, you must respond to them and change your behavior.

In that content marketing is necessary. This are targeted communications post-purchase. Use this opportunity to ensure that customers are happy with your product.

Social media engagement: This involves a combination of customer ratings and reviews as well as sharing their product related experiences via a variety of platforms including Facebook, Twitter, Instagram, Pinterest and YouTube. It also includes platforms that aren't always considered social media such as Amazon (the Granddaddy of ratings and reviews), Yelp and TripAdvisor.

In this sense, getting the most out of the three classic ingredients Tequila Sunrise for Business and all its elements, you should focus completely its great potential on buyer, inviting them to soak up the Sunrise from the Stimulus for your refined coherence of content in social media achieve that sometime within the ZMOT rise of Sunrise Effect in his mind is achieved, realizing that a product carries all the differential characteristics he wants to assume to live them and share, and so from there on prevail and during every moment of truth.

Just thus, the correct combination of Tequila Sunrise for Business will cause:

1.   Full alignment of the objectives of the company:

That will be reflected in the design of your product, where it is important to understand the Stimulus as an instant, which is trigger initial and necessary to work the MOT when your product is presented, and which creates promises in the mind of the prospectus whoever takes as a reference and he wish to consult; since it is through receive the Stimulus that you can understand when the objectives of the company begin to project compliance to the needs you want to satisfy the consumer, therefore the Stimulus itself, is the instant you present and the way disclosed your product to appear and remain as long as possible in their mind and strengthen in the MOT. Product design and audiovisual contents that conform it, they are largely those who maintain that commitment in all the MOT.

2.   A solidly built and well-articulated project:

Conformed from the market study, translated by the brief to its purpose and project level, and based on the opinions containing consumer demands. Which must be strengthened through product design, the raison d'être of the brand, and tone of communication of audiovisual content to the consumer. A way to develop a consistent atmosphere between product attributes and the needs that the prospectus wants to satisfy, to rise these attributes emotionally in his mind accompanying in each of the moments of truth.

3.   A suitable product with shared qualities:

That convinces by its attributes as well as compliance with its central promise, where reality that projects the product is the perception of the prospectus about what he expects to increase their quality of life. Result of a proper direction of the product to meet face to face with the target audience towards making purchasing decision, with the intention of turning it into consumer and the premise of achieving be the only thing that seeks to obtain at all moments of truth: a product with true character, that generates feelings of brand value, and increase your emotional bond, so that the carrying assume their qualities as their own.

In this way, is that you can see the big picture that the Tequila Sunrise for Business pose, and thus converge their correct use towards the critical moments of truth, based on its effect.

It is from launch, when the stimulus (S) is generated, from where it begins to take effect the outcome of Sunrise, which tries to understand the initial moment in that go up and down the valuable attributes of a brand in the mind of the prospectus, causing submerge to consult in the sphere of ZMOT, to achieve make it your consumer against competition (FMOT), looking to get a satisfactory experience (SMOT), and also turn it into a real fan (TMOT); to when use it, make it back on the other side of the sphere of SMOT, getting again enjoy shopping in the FMOT, and with Sunrise up freely endorsing now from the ZMOT.

In other words, how should prepare Sunrise is to be present inside the mind of a prospectus from the time of stimulus, during all interaction, and especially when they want to establish it, so they can become and convert more people in an avid consumer. The best brands are winning in those crucial moments of truth.

A misapplication of Tequila Sunrise for Business, determine a poor outcome of the project and will not cause the effect required to win at all moments of truth. The Tequila Sunrise for Business well combined will achieve in the brand and the product Sunrise Effect to operate in all moments of truth. Therefore a good result of the project as each of the moments of truth, they will support each other.

A brand or product is the material reference and every moment is a sphere of reality to which enters each prospectus or consumer to find the deep needs to assume: the command of his life with the character, the conviction of his actions through the love, and transforming his reality with the attitude that seeks, until a brand grants them in a given product and a faithful content through the right combination, causing the proper effect that sees up in his mind, to select it and extend it to social media.

Sunrise Effect begins when addressing the Stimulus and remains at every Moment Of Truth, and is achieved when it rises in the ZMOT in the consumer's mind.

Basic concept: It's a system to should be efficient throughout the effect that accompanies to the moments of truth, which together make winning to the top brands.

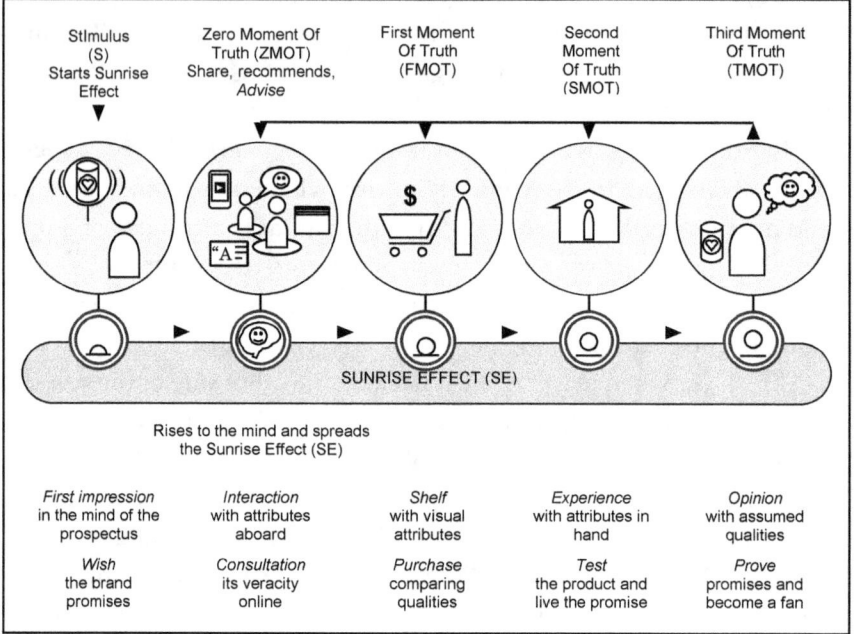

The mental model of purchase. Adapted from: Lecinski, Jim. *Winning the Zero Moment Of Truth.* Illinois: Google Inc., 2011. pp. 16-17. And: http://heidicohen.com/marketing-the-4-moments-of-truth-chart/#sthash.qaOHhTYb.dpuf

Achieve your experience Tequila Sunrise for Business
Let the fiesta begin

Don't limit yourself. You can go as far as your mind lets you. What you believe, remember, you can achieve
MARY KAY ASH
American businesswoman

The recommendation to jump-start the main ingredients and get the experience of Tequila Sunrise for Business, either as start up or company running, it is to develop the disciplines that support it from the base, is about generating a complete renovation.

The preparation of this cocktail requires living up that needs the strong position of the company, the rapidly changing market, and new consumer demands. To do this, pay attention to develop their classic ingredients that must be carefully selected:

1.   Tequila:

Ingredient that corresponds to the administration. It is which effectively represents the strength that requires your company. And as the support that needs to have broad and unique qualities to forever remain standing, from your place of business you must observe the movements of the sector where you stand with your plan to contend with those who are using the perfect combination, and stand firm. Get your company to achieve strong presence since from your startup and your position will be watched by an audience that is eager to find a structure that can to shelter as he likes, and is made with Tequila which belongs to Sunrise.

The liquor served as the first discipline than kicks in, builds the initial organizational basis of any business, from where it develops:

a)   The strategic management process.

b)   And the use of the SWOT analysis: Balancing environments, internal according to the objectives of the organization and external to propose their strategy in the sector of competitiveness, in an appropriate manner, with the approach of "all depends on."

Each company must submit its strategic management process with the development of its mission, vision, philosophy and objectives, supports the name of your firm, corporate identity, and corporate colors, your website should reflect a general reaffirmation of it, which must be as homogeneous as each other to effectively reach to your target audience; that is their projection. And your portfolio should show their technique and its trajectory that raise its category on the market, is the characteristic way to get better positioning than its competition in the industry; that is his strategy.

2.   Orange:

Ingredient that corresponds to marketing. It is which effectively represents the malleability that requires your company. And as the link that needs to have broad and unique qualities to forever adapting to changes consumption, from your place of business you must observe the movements of the market where you stand to know the segment to which you will apply your research and keep that in the sight. Chose well and approach the representative public who is congruent to the purpose you pursue reaching, since you'll be watching for that, the segment from which you will get the best valuable impressions, depends on an accurate projection of the study on contact, to give in mental target from which you can extract the information that consumers want to vent to obtain that which they like demand, and is made with Orange which belongs to Sunrise.

The spill juice, as the second discipline that is activated, strengthens the various connections that will give mobility toward markets, to jump-start:

a)   The marketing management process.

b)   And the marketing mix: Using the 4 P's to analyze the situation and design strategies to achieve profitable organizational objectives and satisfy the real needs of consumers.

Each company must hold its marketing management process in the planning of marketing their services, a high development of balance cost-satisfaction and a detailed direction of the marketing mix towards a satisfactory volume, as a link between company-consumer; that is your advantage. The market planning must be based on the study of its possibilities and the conversion of context to content, driven towards the base for win, that is the consumer, in the consistent way to move the dexterity of marveling at a market in their mobility environment; there it is your competitiveness.

3.   Grenadine:

Ingredient that corresponds to design. It is effectively representing the impact that requires your company. And as the trigger that need extensive and unique qualities to always carry what they are looking to be the prospectus, from your place of operations for the brief, you must observe their movements on the Internet to introduce you to who are interacting in their relentless pursuit of valuation and stay present. Connect to their principles and be consistent with the arguments required by, as each of them will observe you and represents all turned into buyer, and they are about to become the endorsement to recommend and disseminate their deepest needs to get the qualities of what you have created, a global communication that keeps its promises and adds them as part of them, and is made with Grenadine which belongs to Sunrise.

The syrup served as the third discipline than starts, precipitates the plans for representing through image communication to the final consumer, and impels:

a)   The design projects management process.

b)   And the proper use of briefing or design requirements: The ability to define entrepreneurs and members of the company all the objectives and requirements of the project.

Every company should be aware of their design projects management process, based on the fulfillment of its objectives, the project development emphasizing the importance of using the briefing, and overall analysis of its results, involving all those people join in the project with respect to consumer demands; that is their differentiation. Design feature is to be functional and aesthetic, capture the essence of desires that generate consumer loyalty and adapt to a context familiar to him and his life, the mode of excite a consumer within its contextual sphere; that is their innovation.

When a company hits in its sector of competitiveness (their entity), causes adjustments in their mobility environment (their industry) and effects on their spheres of contextuality (their preference); it is because underpins the implementation of the three main disciplines that drive their business, to apply them in their logical sequence from the projection of its dominant process, that is, depending on the process to start a business project the outlook for the other two processes is displayed that consequently take their proper place, adopting the organizational functions that highlights the most important activities that a company requires: to their sector, their environment and context.

Within the development of these disciplines, it is important as second step establish a determinant behavior to spread as a parameter of the entire company:

1. In formulating a consistent distribution of management in the operation of its structure.

That is rounded in strategic management, so that it shows great control of his abilities and great presence of their strengths to the thought of context, in order to reach customers world class whether you work for corporate or promoting their own products. Convincing as firm to the largest audience of a particular market segment, intending to spread globally.

2. When driving a marketing consistent effort in the proposal of their dynamism.

That is supported by strategic marketing so that transfer high conviction pleasurable experiences that give dynamism to the feelings through the stories told, with the intention of achieving a link between the identity of the company, the brand, and the consumer through rapprochement value contents. Tasks to be performed with direct media and specific.

3. When submitting a differentiator design proposal consistent with their communication.

That is focused on image enhancements of the products and services that display its aesthetic and functional aspects of affective-emotional nature with the purpose of sharing the tangible attributes which give sense of belonging and self-satisfaction and manage to fill their deepest needs of reinvention, dominion, security, and connection through direct contact with consumer demands.

Thus, deep inquiry into each development defines a particular intensity in the business result, leading as a third step, the constant demand for talent applied to maximize the proactive diversity that requires each new project, where you must pay attention to:

1.   The strategic performance of the project:

Highlighting in the company an important development of its corporate goals by which to expand their business activities on the performance areas where they are more focused and supported it, leaving a strong evidence of them in each project specifically in the skills that they were targeted (the implementation of strategies), in building their overall performance (the application of competences) and in the effect of the final results (the implementation of innovations), same elements that reflect its vision and mission, consistently with the important role they play in the market, and the good use of their own design process. The development of briefing is paramount in adapting to changes in obtaining information regardless of the type of project.

2.   The competitive environment analysis:

Each company must show great attention to changes in consumption that could generate the results of the brand or product designed. Their analysis will add the relevant competences and decrease unnecessary under the conditions of briefing, also examines the dose of the ingredients of Sunrise for Business that were implemented to the project. Whether for new launches, when requiring renovation, or adding new elements of communication, these tools play an important role first to identify the best solution to your requirements and then to see how successful was this choice. Each product has certain qualities that must be renewed, the fact overcome them makes compete with renewed mettle increasingly adapted to their context.

3.   The innovations applied to products:

Innovations are an important tool for products and services as a great consumer appeal. Although the needs of each product are varied and also tend to be aimed at different market segments, only those relevant changes in the products are those that help them compete, aspect which shows that however small or large it is a change, there is behind a study that supports its effectiveness and why sometimes projects last months. Applied innovations will allow highlight how satisfied consumer preferences.

Regardless of specialization in any of the areas of design performance, in the different companies must employ the three performances mentioned in the most appropriate manner from the status of renewal of a product, namely, that depending on the improvements required for each brand it is makes sense the implementation of the strategy, innovation, and competitiveness as well as their level of performance in every product.

And thus as the fourth step is required a high degree of professionalism:

1. Putting in place the strategies:

a) The directives, that command the correct trajectory of design project in the company.

b) Of communication, that intensify product opportunities in the market.

c) The visual, allowing mental association of functional-emotional-aesthetical appealing to the consumer.

2. By providing competitiveness in:

a) The way the business conduct is administered to realize the project, keeping a customer, and impact the consumer to strengthen itself in the market.

b) The ability to manage marketing to get the project, give it capabilities that will position in the market and achieve their effects on the consumer.

c) The perspicacity into the use of design to formulate emotional atmospheres that cause change and to cope with the changes achieved market trends required by the consumer.

3. Accompanying opportunely with innovations:

a) In the administration, since allow better methods emerge for efficiency and effectiveness of the business.

b) In marketing, when formulating the most attractive conditions for global communication about the project.

c) In design, based on new connotations that are not present and will be unique characteristics of the product.

Basic Concept: The process of managing business projects requires the joint work of the administration, marketing and design. As strategic forces, competitive advantages and differentials innovations, at the corporate level, management, functional and operational.

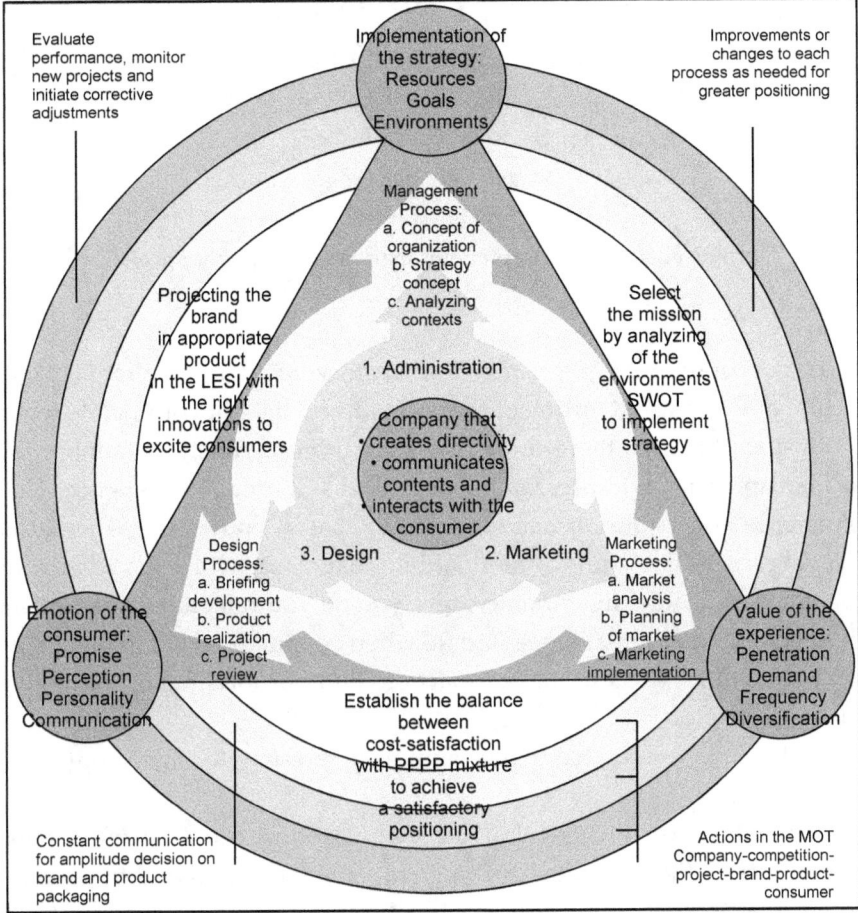

Evaluate performance, monitor new projects and initiate corrective adjustments

Implementation of the strategy: Resources Goals Environments

Improvements or changes to each process as needed for greater positioning

Management Process:
a. Concept of organization
b. Strategy concept
c. Analyzing contexts

Projecting the brand in appropriate product in the LESI with the right innovations to excite consumers

Select the mission by analyzing of the environments SWOT to implement strategy

1. Administration

Company that
• creates directivity
• communicates contents and
• interacts with the consumer

Design Process:
a. Briefing development
b. Product realization
c. Project review

3. Design

2. Marketing

Marketing Process:
a. Market analysis
b. Planning of market
c. Marketing implementation

Emotion of the consumer:
Promise Perception Personality Communication

Value of the experience:
Penetration Demand Frequency Diversification

Establish the balance between cost-satisfaction with PPPP mixture to achieve a satisfactory positioning

Constant communication for amplitude decision on brand and product packaging

Actions in the MOT Company-competition-project-brand-product-consumer

The three management processes in the company. They are cyclical functions of business management to achieve the objectives.

A bite of decorated
The orange and cherry

The decoration has a great role to be to your liking at first sight, to accompany a pleasant tasting of the cocktail, and delight your palate when you taste at the end; these three forms are used to generally identify the cocktail and remain impressed in your mind as a unique experience. That experience you rejoice, becomes unforgettable in your mind when after enjoying their tastes run to the final bite that closes with a flourish your personalized reality, in summary, tells you all you remember the content since you saw her initial presentation, when you ingested completely, and until you felt its effect to make it part of you appropriating it you with a bite given to life.

So I want you to have this summary present to start your own combination.

Remember, to fully develop the Tequila Sunrise for Business must concentrate all the elements required and serve the ingredients in the right order, that way you'll have on hand the arguments to control the preparation and effect. So far, your party is just beginning.

To continue, you will know the description of the bite that you require to keep aware, is a review of the Tequila Sunrise for Business, the idea of this is assimilate the main components to keep into mind and make run all needs the cocktail, I strongly suggest you pay attention to this extract to assimilate all development effectively and make your business a more paradisiacal and lasting scenery for enjoying.

1. The tumbler:

Let's start by make it clear that to achieve the business you imagine first you need to have a place from where you will develop the processes governing ideology for your business. That place should reflect the solidity with which you plant in a sector and security with which you spread to the world.

The tumbler is the container of all your "professional business structure;" is the material and intellectual capital, that is, your physical facilities and your most select personnel with which you will achieve your every move and get what you want to achieve. And as the support where you must pour ingredients to develop their best aspects, needs to have broad and unique qualities to receive the combined, contain the correct dose, and share its effect inside and outside, it must be large enough in order to be prepared for all the activities that generated inside and be specially distributed to contain a correct workflow. Therefore get ready with the right tumbler which it is the body of your business, where your capital will action your "business plan."

Your tumbler is the physic structure of your company which has presence from its location and represents your company wherever you present, should be adequate, portentous, and transparently visible.

2. Ice cubes:

Thus we come to ice, that is the business intention of wanting to win and do win, you lead to the consumer. Intention arising from the high command and magnifies on their way to go characteristically shaping the skills with which you count in each ingredient. At every instant you make your corresponding activities, collaborate with doing work that intention, that is shared throughout the team through the flow line intellectual production and is forming a uniform particle cumulus, which interpenetrate as part of the cocktail to go by cooling the mixture to reach the material realization.

Ice cubes has long range as it should be capable enough to spread to those who will complement, the "representative segment" through "market research;" will builds the scenarios that you want to reach and unstoppable way with you face your reality.

The temper that gives the intention always is reflected in "your faithful consumer" containing the mixture of the action elaborated and directed by your professional structure, with the requested action and now to the expectation of your representative segment. Cumulus that must now be translated especially well, exceeding expectations for both culminating in proper cooling of the combined.

Your ice are the intention to grant to each of the elements that you develop in your company, and that is reflected especially in the translation of "briefing" as a reflection of wanting to win that leads the consumer and is collected from he. They should be the most complete, crystalline and cold.

3.   Tequila:

As the first active ingredient in the Sunrise, you must pour the "administration" with which you have to create and capture all your plans. If you do not know why your company does not work as you want and want to have everything in order, the configuration of the mission, vision, and values that underpin your business must change to project as a stronger support base. To do so requires a solid "business plan" that is the structure with the goals of your company, only if you know how your company is structured and how it works from the ground up to its ultimate impact, is that you have total control over what you have, to build and get to what you want to achieve. There are no limits to achieve your projects, you can change, improve, and make the most complete and firm administration can imagine, just knowing. If you know what and how is in detail that what you're holding, you will understand how easy it is to operate the ideal structure necessary for your company, to raise corporate objectives and strategy use homogeneously inside and outside your company.

That way you manage your projection involving in the analysis of their internal and external environments "SWOT", with the further involve all your human capital and talent, invite all participants within the sector to compete, level on which first you should take into account the public that is the main spectator of each movement showing your company. Here the *presence-expectation* urge arises, where the public expects to receive benefits of what sells the presence they are seeing stand.

These processes must develop and maintain strong support from your "corporate identity" this is the visual representation of your company that projects formally planted into the sector their behavior and mentality sets that is directed to your target audience. Designing your corporate identity should be based on an analysis of all your strategic process, where your mission, vision, values and philosophy construct the form of visual communication as will see your company and will relate an identity supported by the strength of "character" that itself projects.

Your tequila should be the structural basis of your company, represents the presence at the sector and your target audience. The best tonic home.

4.   Orange:

With this active ingredient of the cocktail, you should show how you go develop characteristics the product or service you want bring to market more suitable for consumption. All business projects must be based on knowledge of what the market demands, fresh information obtained from the target audience will be whoever gets enjoyment and judge the qualities of your product. Better knowledge that you can get to collect feelings and incorporate them into business goals your company is from "the representative segment" chosen that will throw the first and most faithful firsthand evidence containing these requested features. To do this you must apply a malleable "market research," from this paper meet the requirements the profile of respondents have created, results among which especially you know important details that your target market prefers about the product and its attributes. You must know precisely the ways and moments when your market feels more familiar with your product and also at what point is more susceptible to appropriate it as his so that at some point be able to enjoy it and can satisfy with it. The study should know how the consumer feels what will be your product.

Knowing the market is a revealing point. You must learn to project the appropriate market management actions of your company to activate the "4 P's" that allow direct interaction towards the target market and obtaining their response to stimuli that affect their satisfaction. It will permeate the way you should approach the project translated into items and audiovisual content from the company to the prospectus; the objective of the "marketing" is fulfilled by conserving valuable exchange *experience-satisfaction* in renewals of the brand on the market requirements. When the target market gets its first successful experience as a result of the first exchange.

The strategic sense of marketing must move through your brand that is the visual representation that inherits in a certain part the character of your company and linked with feelings towards the target market, constituting its values and its own identity as a brand. It is essential to design the "brand identity" will require your product based on it will establish the sentimental contact requests your target market thereby will acquire a certain price, it may be subject to better promoted and may be placed in a square for distribution, so it will be propitious to communicate "love" that creates identity and loyalty.

Your orange must be the malleable link to your company, the identity between the objectives and requirements of the target market. The natural juice concentrates the flavors.

5.   Grenadine:

When pouring this syrup you must capture consumer preferences, and move them as "study results." With them you will reflect the characteristics of their emotions, based on their translation and adaptation, will have on hand all the elements that will provide your product with the visual possibilities that will align to the objectives of the company to composing both the DNA as form personality of the product. You get a result that shares features of the company and gives the desirable nature of the final consumer; the translation of the study results should communicate them scrupulously. The key is to apply what you know, and improve what you have learned, so that empower. To do this you have to make proper use of "briefing", this important document of drafting your product requirements, is of invaluable assistance with which translate from concepts, into functional, aesthetic and emotional attributes all the demands that a consumer could want, based on their careful monitoring is that you will get a product well contextualized to the greatest extent should be satisfactory and if possible should exceed expectations, to be reflected in increased sales and product recommendation to put facing the consumer.

And for this must turn the design projects managing process, to extend actual parameters of the project with the purpose of circulating the constant *effect-emotion* in the mind of the consumer. When it is already a fact that the effects of the preparation have begun to rise in the mind of the prospectus as attractive to his life that is causing that satisfaction. Much so that based on company objectives and translation of the brief must implement the strategy of "design" through its strategic process, by addressing the Level, Environment, Strategy and Implementation of the project "(LESI)" towards renewal or continuation, based on the promise and product perception, nurtured with consumer demands; to highlight its values and qualities and provide it with its own personality and good communication. Consider the analysis of the results.

All this development should result in your "product design" that through acquiring its functional, aesthetic and emotional attributes will be established as the focal point that embodies the full essence of projected goals and requested features helping to determine the purchase. You must work to fulfill the central promise of the product, keep in touch with the needs of the prospectus and attend the perception of the product facing consumer's emotions to turn in "attitude."

Your grenadine must be the forceful contact from your company, the emotional attributes of the product to the consumer. The syrup that triggers the impact on the mind.

6.   Starting Sunrise Effect:

You should get to successfully give birth the desire of owning your product and its promised emotional attributes in the greatest amount of prospectus, during the different moments of truth from the "Stimulus", the one who emits an item or content counting a valuable and true story about your "product"; is from that "instant" created in time, which can be from the launch or subsequently, that the Sunrise Effect must be maintained as constant excitement and present inside the mind of the prospectus.

If your conformation of Tequila Sunrise for Business is correct, surely it must cause have lasting effects on the prospectus and direct at every moment of truth "starting Sunrise Effect"; will be effective if it remains faithful from the stimulus until it raises to the mind of the prospectus, taking place in there the Sunrise that checks their promised attributes.

Your Effect should be a catalyst for your company and shocking to the prospectus, to approve at every moment a good, very good, better, excellent, a ha!

7.   Raising Sunrise Effect:

With the Sunrise Effect barely tackled in the mind of the prospectus, must get their immediate response motivating to consult online about the product to find the promise not yet checked but then possibly will fill his need to possess it, passing one by one the moments of truth until they confirm their qualities awakened from the instant when happens the Stimulus and through an increase in emotions. From "ZMOT, FMOT, SMOT, to the TMOT."

To do this every MOT should keep and what better to increase consumer confidence despite the presence of other products, until convince them that the acquisition that will make or has made is what they expected and of their full satisfaction for endorse it.

Your MOT should be able to "raising the Sunrise Effect" up in the mind of the prospectus and subsequent consumer. They should build a pleasant conviviality when invite to tasting the Sunrise to the prospectus and consumers.

8.   Spreading Sunrise Effect:

When finally now the consumer of product has gone through all the moments of truth successfully and is fully convinced of the product and its emotional attributes come true for satisfying their need, then must become in an endorsement to go recommending the same product.

To do so when consumers return to ZMOT must now give the opinion from their experience with the product and advise in interaction with a new prospectus who wants to query, and with the power of Sunrise Effect accomplished in the mind of now endorsement, this person can convert to another loyal consumer, thereby, "spreading the Sunrise Effect."

The Sunrise Effect must have the quality to cause a unique impression from the first arrival at the "ZMOT" in its consultation, for be the same in the second visit, now to be shared by those who should make known the ultimate party that generates taste the Tequila Sunrise for Business without knowing that it is contained into a final product.

And to have effect on your company develop it properly:

KEYS:	CONTAINS:	TRANSLATE TO:
Tumbler:	Your professional structure	Business plan
Ice cubes:	Your representative segment	Market research
Ice cubes:	Your faithful consumer	Briefing
INGREDIENT:	ACTIVE FORM:	REPRESENTATIVE PATTERN:
Tequila:	Management (SWOT)	Corporate identity & Enterprise
Orange:	Marketing (4 P's)	Brand & Contents video
Grenadine:	Design (LESI)	Brand identity & Product
TRIGGER in:	REFLECTED in:	SATISFY when:
Starting SE:	Stimulus: Moment + Product	Sunrise is introduced to mind
Raising SE:	ZMOT, FMOT, SMOT, TMOT	Customer become endorsement
Spreading SE:	Return to ZMOT to share	Convert more consumers
IT OBTAINED AS A RESULT		
Development of Tequila Sunrise for Business		

Note that properly prepare the Tequila Sunrise for Business will contain the specific characteristics of each company, reflected in the congruent construction of the product design and Stimulus, so that these two elements contain the qualities of Tequila Sunrise, and are projecting the emotional benefits to obtain the Sunrise Effect at crucial Moments Of Truth, wherein the Sunrise Effect will rise one by one on the consumer's mind until the effect of the purchased product is up in the minds of consumers when the emotional benefits promised by the product are checked and are finally endorsed by him, causing recommend the product, sharing to a new prospect already tested the Sunrise Effect, who certainly also will check, will rise to his mind and become a loyal consumer more.

The constant imperative has always been to obtain consumer information, only now stands first, the moment of which should be taken, is from ZMOT, and then is the challenge of how to do it well, attending the emotional benefits that rise to the mind of consumer to incorporate to take effect in new products that promote and impact on consumer habits.

In summary, (quoted in Taylor & Shaw, 1990) "there are three types of companies, those that make things happen, those who watch things happen and those who wonder what happened." (Anonymous)

It has been a pleasure for me having prepared this cocktail, you've come to the bar, and have enjoyed it as a prelude to the party that proposes the Matrix, mastering in business. Now is the time to prepare it well chilled and put it to take effect, to bring up the sun in the mind your next similar, that instead of turning him only into your consumer, be a collaborator more of your business to expand them for the purpose that you win and make him win in the day by day to get what you want to achieve.

This is the preparation of a delicious combination of three ancestral ingredients converted into classics, to be efficient and win in business as is required on a large scale and attract consumers of the international market, which everybody should taste.

Cocktail that depends on you to dominate it, and if you allow it from now on, you can to prepare with mastery and at deeper levels. So that it helps you to discover how you can achieve what you ultimately look for in you, get the Sunrise. With which I suggest the following: *In your excitement to succeed, look at each previous step from the future scenario and build it on your path.*

Work in a network
We are all Tequila, show character

I would like to see anyone be able to achieve their dreams, and that's what this organization does
SERGEI BRIN
Russian American computer scientist, internet entrepreneur, and philanthropist

Basic concept: Our organs, in connection with the universal consciousness are capable of flowing energy of the universe that we contain to manifest reality and to recycle the energy contained to reconsider our patterns.

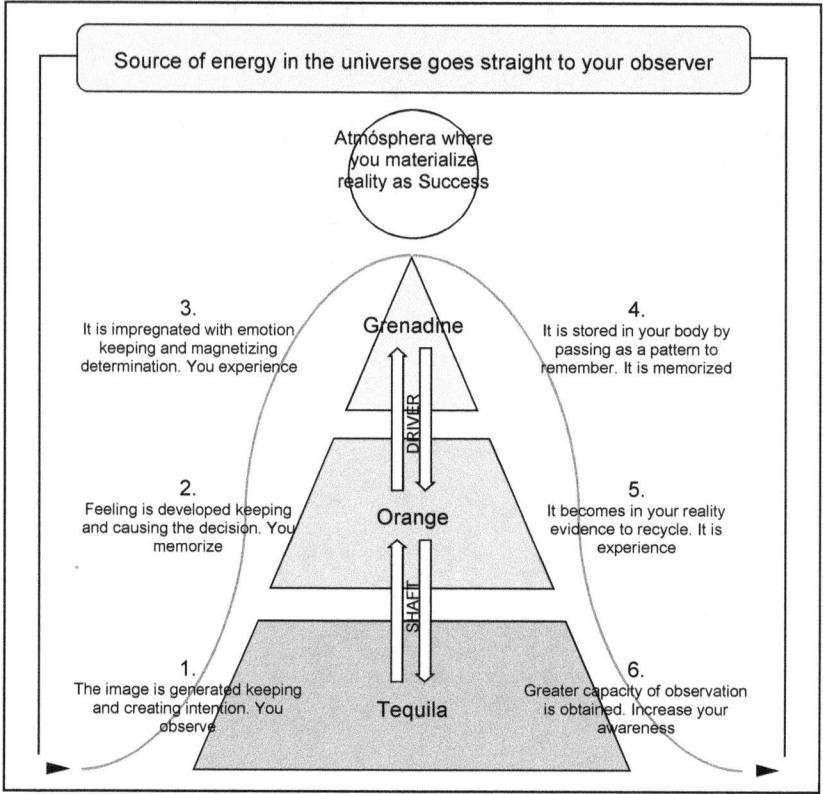

The pyramid of creating success through the Sunrise. Based on the observation of the human body and its contact with the universe, their reactions and manifestation of reality. Mind, body and consciousness.

Increase your connection
We are all Orange, just love

Build something 100 people love, not something 1 million people kind of like
BRIAN CHESKY
American Internet entrepreneur

Basic concept: Manifesting reality in business is based on the approach of the energy of the universe: 1 master processes, 2 empower their mark with identity, brand and product, 3 provoke character, love and attitude, in the minds of consumers.

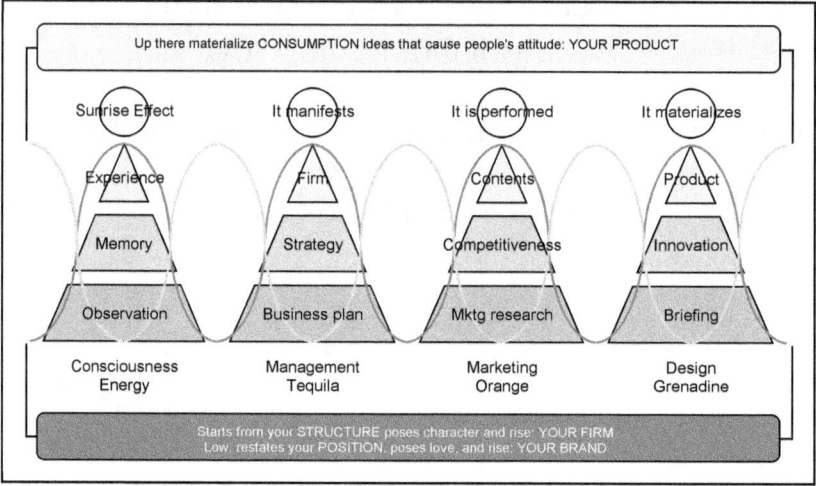

The flow of Tequila Sunrise for Business through the pyramid of success. Based on the observation of the universe and its manifestation in business. Mind, consumers and businesses.

Make your business exponential
We are all Grenadine, have attitude

Don't be afraid to change the model
REED HASTINGS
American businessman, philanthropist and CEO

As human beings born on this planet, each of us, we have the right to live in a space suitable for our personal development, and also generate a knowledge for the development of humanity in general. Maybe you enjoy it, maybe you do not have any, or you do not have and develop both, however, whatever that does not mean that we cannot achieve them. And you can make it possible, through the proper use of the whole set of elements to which the total control of your emotions alludes, which is also linked to these other functions of our body to act its totality.

Basic Concept: The set of triads that project to a company to success in business is dumped in a circuit working in unison. Become aware of the whole picture put into action your circuit.

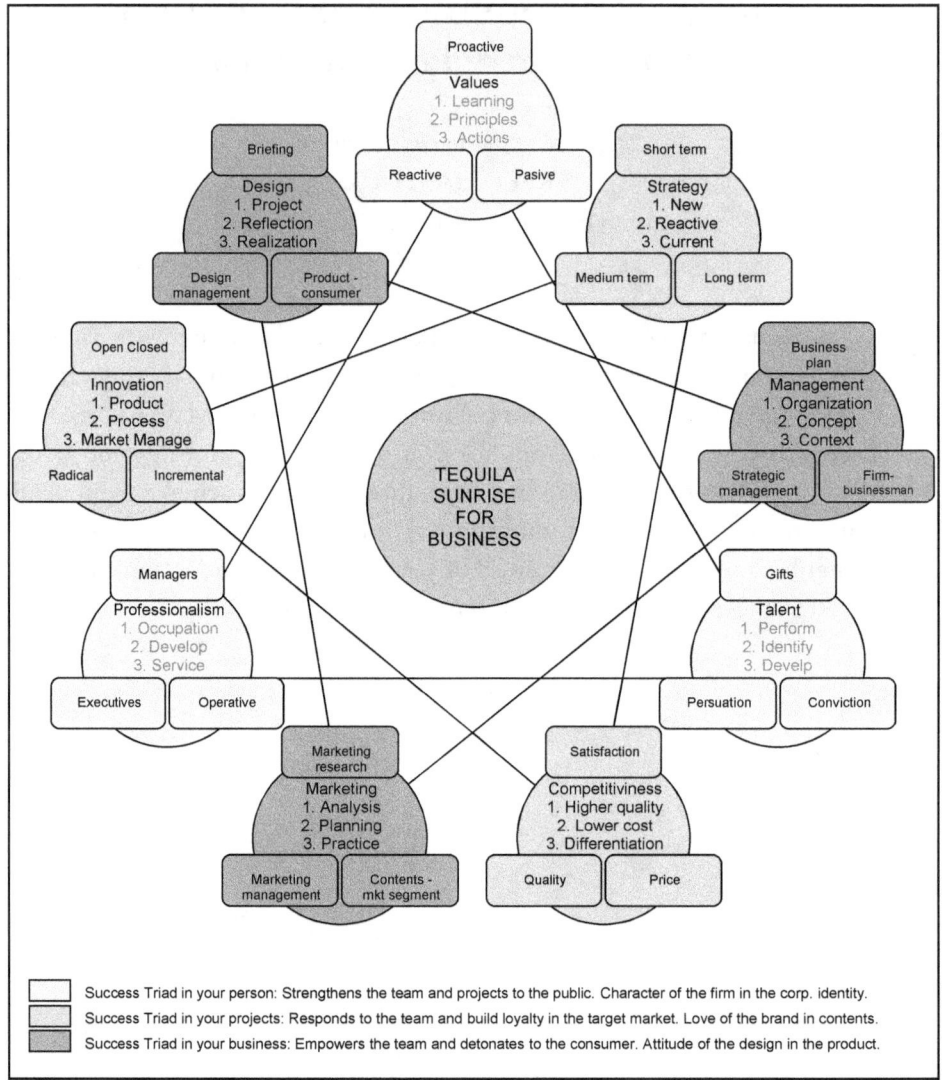

Tequila Sunrise for Business success triads. Based on the observation of the universe and its manifestation in business. Mind, consumers and businesses.

Bibliography

1.   AMA.org. (2004, October). *About AMA.* Retrieved July 30, 2013, from Definition of Marketing:
https://www.ama.org/AboutAMA/Pages/Definition-of-Marketing.aspx

2.   AMA.org. (2014). *Dictionary AMA.* Retrieved October 31, 2014, from Marketing mix:
https://www.ama.org/resources/pages/dictionary.aspx?dLetter=M

3.   Argote, L., & Ingram, P. (2000, May). Knowledge transfer: A basis for competitive advantage in firms. *82*(1), 150-169.

4.   Artiux. (2016). *Design Management in Design Companies of Mexico City.* USA.

5.   Baena, V. (2011). *Fundamentos de marketing: entorno, consumidor, estrategia e investigación comercial [Fundamentals of Marketing: environment, consumer and trade research strategy].* Barcelona, Spain: Editorial UOC.

6.   Berry, T. (2014, October 13). *Soyentrepreneur.com.* (T. Berry, Editor) Retrieved October 13, 2014, from 8 pasos para escribir tu plan de negocios [8 steps to write your business plan]:
http://www.soyentrepreneur.com/27518-8-pasos-para-escribir-tu-plan-de-negocios.html

7.   Bezos, J. (2013, September 13th). Four Peaks: My interview with Jeff Bezos. Seattle, Washington, USA: Youtube. Retrieved from https://www.youtube.com/watch?v=vhDRBPCOxmA

8.   Bonsiepe, G. (1999). *Del objeto a la interfase: Mutaciones del diseño [Of the object to the interface: Design Mutations].* Buenos Aires, Argentina: Ediciones Infinito.

9.   Branson, R. (2007, March). Richard Branson Life at 30,000 feet. Monterey, California, USA: Youtube. Retrieved from https://www.ted.com/talks/richard_branson_s_life_at_30_000_feet?language=es#t-37883

10.   Brant, J., & Lohse, S. (2014). *The open innovation model.* Paris, France: International Chamber of Commerce.

11.   Bruce, M., & Bessant, J. (2002). *Design in business. Strategic Innovation Through Design.* London, England: Financial Times-Prentice

Hall.

12.   Bruce, M., Cooper, R., & Vazquez, D. (1999). *Effective design management for small businesses* (Vol. 20). Manchester, United Kingdom: Design Studies.

13.   Buffett, W. (2013, July 2th). Warren Buffett speaks with Florida University. Gainesville, Florida, USA: Youtube. Retrieved from https://www.youtube.com/watch?v=2MHIcabnjrA&ebc=ANyPxKoAX iutNLg2xHQ53OOTx-eLB5VoY6TU6kRWKoM_sTpQ0UiWSqLS9MaFWq22W1gYHNzlDNF82 5YoLLaNKjRGr15c6W_94g

14.   Castillo, C., & Bond, F. O. (1987). *The university of Chicago spanish-english english-spanish dictionary*. USA: Pocket Books.

15.   Chaves, N. (2001). *El oficio de diseñar. Propuesta a la conciencia crítica de los que comienzan [The profession of designing. Proposal to critical awareness of those who begin]*. Barcelona, Spain: GG Diseño.

16.   Chiavenato, I. (2001). *Introducción a la teoría general de la administración [Introduction to general management theory]*. Mexico City, Mexico: McGraw-Hill.

17.   Coca Carasila, A. M. (2008, May-August). El concepto de Marketing: pasado y presente [Marketing Concept: Past and Present]. (J. Fuenmayor, Ed.) *Revista de Ciencias Sociales [Journal of Social Sciences]*, 393-395.

18.   Cohen, H. (2013, June 27). *Marketing: The 4 Moments of Truth [Chart]*. (L. Aronson, Editor, WebFaction, Producer, & Aweber) Retrieved December 01, 2014, from Marketing's 4 moments of truth defined: http://heidicohen.com/marketing-the-4-moments-of-truth-chart/#sthash.qaOHhTYb.dpuf

19.   Colmenares Grünberger, O. (1992). *Administración Estratégica: Casos de Empresas Mexicanas [Strategic Management: Case Mexican Companies]*. Mexico City, Mexico: Edamex.

20.   Condusef. (2013). *Empresario PyME como usuarios de servicios financieros [Businessman SMEs as the users of financial services]*. Retrieved October 10, 2014, from Plan de negocios y cómo hacerlo [Business Plan and how to do]: http://www.condusef.gob.mx/index.php/empresario-pyme-como-usuarios-de-servicios-financieros/119-plan-de-negocios-y-como-hacerlo

21.   Consejo Regulador del Tequila [Tequila Regulatory Council].
(2013, November 1st). *http://www.crt.org.mx*. Retrieved from Información
Estadística [Statistical information]:
http://www.crt.org.mx/EstadisticasCRTweb/
22.   Contreras, J. (2001). *Administración estratégica [Strategic
Management]*. Mexico City, Mexico: Universidad Nacional Autónoma de
México.
23.   Daniels, W. R. (2000, Spring). Meetings build strategic
relationships. *Design Management Journal, 11*(2), 63-71.
24.   De Jong, J., Vanhaverbeke, W., Kalvet, T., & Chesbrough, H.
(2008). *Policies for open innovation: Theory, framework and cases.* Helsinki,
Finland: Research project funded by Vision Era-Net.
25.   Donis Dondis, A. (1992). *La sintaxis de la imagen. Introducción al
alfabeto visual [A Primer of Visual Literacy]*. Mexico City, Mexico: GG
Diseño.
26.   Droste, M. (1991). *Bauhaus 1919-1933*. Berlin, Germany: Editorial
Archive and Museum of Design Bauhaus.
27.   EducaMarketing. (2005). *Guía para realizar una Investigación de
Mercados [Guide to perform a Market Research]*. (U. Extremadura, Ed.)
Retrieved November 01, 2014, from Área de Comercialización e
Investigación de Mercados [Department of Marketing and Market
Research]:
http://educamarketing.unex.es/Docs/guias/Gu%C3%ADa%20realizaci
%C3%B
28.   Ellison, L. (2013, February 23th). Exclusive interview of Larry
Ellison - ceo of oracle corp. India: Youtube. Retrieved from
https://www.youtube.com/watch?v=OLahcEI--
2E&ebc=ANyPxKonJFxix38yRNgpp6BD6D_sjeZbc3bgETS8Xsme3Ugj9j5
qbCAtg5BcpOm4f_NUaLlil8A4sOqOrtGvusu_08ZNMDsXzg
29.   Enríquez Morán, C. (2013, October 29). *Forbes.com.mx*. Retrieved
from 4 secretos básicos del marketing para PyMEs [4 basic secrets of
marketing for SMEs]: http://www.forbes.com.mx/4-secretos-basicos-
del-marketing-para-pymes/
30.   Etimonline.com. (2014). *Online Etymology Diccionary*. (D. C.
Buglione, Editor, D. McCormack, Producer, & Sponsored Words)
Retrieved October 26, 2014, from Market:

http://www.etymonline.com/index.php?allowed_in_frame=0&search=market&searchmode=none

31.   Filson, A., & Lewis, A. (2000). Barriers between design and business strategy. *Design Management Journal, 11*(4), 48-52.

32.   Fischer De la Vega, L., & Espejo Callado, J. (2004). *Mercadotecnia [Marketing]* (3rd ed.). Mexico City, Mexico: Mc Graw Hill.

33.   Fisher De la Vega, L. (1988). *Mercadotecnia [Marketing]*. Mexico City, Mexico: Interamericana.

34.   Free-management-ebooks.com. (2013). *Ansoff Matrix. Strategy Skills*. Warwickshire, United Kingdom: free-management-ebooks.com.

35.   Frías, J. (2004, February 14). Administración del diseño [Design management]. (A. Pérez Iragorri, Ed.) *a! Diseño*(67), 57-59. Retrieved Noviembre 10, 2007, from http://www.a.com.mx

36.   Fuentes, V. (2013, January 10). Las marcas más poderosas [The most powerful brands]. (J. F. López, Ed.) *Poder y Negocios [Power and Business magazine]*, 1, 28-32, 34
http://www.mediasolutions.com.mx/ncpop.asp?n=201310090057014801&t=.

37.   García Padilla, V. M. (2014). *Introducción a las finanzas [Introduction to Finance]*. Mexico City, Mexico: Grupo Editorial Patria.

38.   Gates, B. (2013, May 10th). Buffett & Gates on Success. Seattle, Washington, USA. Retrieved from
https://www.youtube.com/watch?v=ldPh0_zEykU

39.   Gombrich, E. H. (1999). *La historia del arte [The history of art]*. Mexico City, Mexico: Conaculta-Editorial Diana.

40.   González, C. (2004, February 14). Design Bureau. Entrevista a Carlos González Nacif [Design Bureau. Interview with Carlos González Nacif]. (A. Pérez Iragorri, Ed.) *a! Diseño*(67), 41-47. Retrieved september 16, 2008, from http://www.a.com.mx

41.   Grefé, R. (1997). *Design culture. An anthology of writing from the AIGA journal of graphic design*. (S. Heller, Ed.) New York, USA: Allwort Press.

42.   Guijosa, V., & Frías, J. (2006, January 15). Administración del diseño [Design management]. (A. Pérez Iragorri, Ed.) *a! Diseño*(77), 77-79. Retrieved August 23, 2007, from http://www.a.com.mx

43.   Hauser, A. (1978). *Historia social de la literatura y del arte [Social*

history of literature and art] (Vol. 1). Madrid, Spain: Guadarrama Punto Omega.

44.   Hill, C. W., & Jones, G. R. (2005). *Administración estratégica. Un enfoque integrado [Strategic Management: An Integrated Approach].* Mexico City, Mexico: McGraw Hill Interamericana.

45.   Idologie.com. (2012). *Proceso [Process].* (J. Olguín, Producer) Retrieved October 15, 2014, from mapa/breif [map/briefing]: http://www.idologie.com/proceso.html

46.   Iduarte, J., & Zarza, M. (2004). *La administración del diseño en micro pequeñas y medianas empresas mexicanas [The design management in micro small and medium Mexican companies].* Autonomous University of Estado de México, Faculty of Architecture and Design. Toluca: UAEM. Retrieved 07 10, 2006, from http://www.dis.uia.mx/conference/2005/HTMs-PDFs/AdmondelDisenoenEmpresas.pdf

47.   Isern, A. (2003). *Guía creativity 2003: el diseño y la comunicación en la gestión empresarial [Creativity Guide 2003: design and communication in business management].* Barcelona, Spain: Guía Creativity.

48.   J., Boyd, H., O., W., & Larreché, J. (2007). *Administración de marketing. Un enfoque en la toma estratégica de decisiones. [Marketing Management: A Strategic Decision-Making Approach].* Mexico City, Mexico: Mc Graw Hil Interamericana.

49.   Jeffrey, K. R., & Hunt, D. (1985, Janauary). Design in small manufacturing companies in Scotland. *6*(1), 18-24.

50.   Kaplan, A. M. (2014, August). European management and European business schools: Insights from the History of Business Schools. (M. Haenlein, Ed.) *European Management Journal, 32*(4), 529-534.

51.   Kirwin, R. (2004, February 14). Marca la diferencia [Mark the difference]. (A. Pérez Iragorri, Ed.) *a! Diseño*(67), 49. Retrieved April 23, 2007, from http://www.a.com.mx

52.   Knight, P. (2014, June 14th). Stanford Graduate School of Business Graduation Remarks by Phil Knight, MBA '62. Palo Alto, California, USA: Youtube. Retrieved from https://www.youtube.com/watch?v=nRN9FwWQY8w

53.   Kotler, P. (2009). *Dirección de mercadotecnia [Marketing Management].* Mexico City, Mexico: Prentice Hall.

54.   Kotler, P., & Amstrong, G. (2003). *Fundamentos de marketing [Fundamentals of Marketing]*. Mexico City, Mexico: Pearson Education.

55.   Kunst, M. (1995, March-April). Notas para una filosofía del diseño [Notes for a design philosophy]. (L. Moreno, Ed.) *De Diseño, 1*(3), 8-9.

56.   La Nación. (2008, June 01). *Joan Costa: El diseño socializa el conocimiento [Joan Costa: Design socializes knowledge]*. Retrieved November 07, 2014, from Enfoques [Approaches]: http://www.lanacion.com.ar/1017188-joan-costa-el-diseno-socializa-el-conocimiento

57.   Lamb, C., Hair, J., & McDaniel, C. (2011). *Marketing*. Mexico City, Mexico: Cengage Learning.

58.   Lawrence, P. (1996). Inc. Magazine's George Gendron on design. *@issue. The Journal of Business and Design, 2*(1), 2-5.

59.   Lecinski, J. (2011). *ZMOT Ebook: Winning the Zero Moment of Truth*. Illinois, Chicago, USA: Google Inc.

60.   Levy, A. R. (1981). *Planeamiento estratégico [Strategic Planning]*. Buenos Aires, Argentina: Ediciones Macchi.

61.   Licko, Z. (2002, Spring). 'It's not a problem of being a woman in a man's world. It's being a type designer in a world that gives little recognition to this art form'. (J. L. Walters, Ed.) *Eye magazine, 11*(43), http://eyemagazine.com/feature/article/reputations-zuzana-licko.

62.   Lupton, E., & Abott, M. J. (1994). *El abc de la Bauhaus y la teoría del diseño [ABC's of the Bauhaus: Bauhaus and Design Theory]*. Barcelona, Spain: GG Diseño.

63.   Mintzberg, H., Brian, J., & Voyer, J. (1997). *El proceso estratégico. Conceptos, contextos y casos [The Strategy Process: Concepts, Context, Cases]*. Mexico City, Mexico: Prentice Hall Hispanoamericana.

64.   Mono, D., Rivers, C., & Dowdy, C. (2006). *Identidad corporativa: del brief a la solución final. [Branding: From Brief to Finished Solution]*. Barcelona, Spain: GG Diseño.

65.   Mullins, J., Boyd, H., O., W., & Larreché, J. (2007). *Administración de marketing. Un enfoque en la toma estratégica de decisiones [Marketing Management: A Strategic Decision-Making Approach]*. Mexico City, Mexico: Mc Graw Hil Interamericana.

66.   Munch Galindo, L. (2009). *Fundamentos de administración*

[Management foundations]. Mexico City, Mexico: Trillas.

67.   Muñoz, P. (2007, September 20). X_Design. Estrategias para llegar a grandes clientes [Strategies to reach large customers]. (A. Pérez Iragorri, Ed.) *a! Diseño*(86), 30-37. Retrieved December 04, 2007, from http://www.a.com.mx

68.   Musk, E. (2014, May 16th). Elon Musk USC Commencement Speech | USC Marshall School of Business Undergraduate Commencement 2014. Los Angeles, California, USA: Youtube. Retrieved from https://www.youtube.com/watch?v=e7Qh-vwpYH8

69.   Myownbusiness.org. (2013, December 12). *Session 2: The Business Plan*. Retrieved October 13, 2014, from What is a business plan?: http://www.myownbusiness.org/espanol/s2/#1

70.   Nafinsa. (2009). *www.nafin.gob.mx*. (NacionalFinanciera, Ed.) Retrieved from 13 Pasos para Hacer tu Plan de Negocios [13 Steps to Make Your Business Plan]: www.nafin.gob.mx/portalnf/get?file=/pdf/otros/TRECE-PASOS.pdf

71.   O'Reilly, J. (2002). *Sin briefing: proyectos personales de diseñadores gráficos [No Brief: Graphic Designers' Personal Projects]*. Spain: Index Book.

72.   Olson, E., Slater, S., & Cooper, R. (2000). Managing design for competitive advantage. *Design Managament Journal, 11*(4), 10-17.

73.   Organization for Economic Co-operation and Development. (2005). *Oslo Manual: Guidelines for Collecting and Interpreting Innovation Data*. European Commission: OECD Publishing.

74.   Page, L. (12th de December de 2013). 2014 Breakthrough Prize Ceremony: Michael Hall and Larry Page. Mountain view, California, USA: Youtube. Obtenido de https://www.youtube.com/watch?v=gNZKtRjvrvo

75.   Pérez Iragorri, A. (Ed.). (2007, March 20). La psicología del color en el producto [The psychology of color in the product]. *a! Diseño*(83), 59. Retrieved July 13, 2007, from http://www.a.com.mx

76.   Phoenixnewtimes. (2015). *http://www.phoenixnewtimes.com*. Retrieved from arts/the-biltmore-original-tequila-sunrise: http://www.phoenixnewtimes.com/arts/the-biltmore-original-tequila-sunrise-6570176

77.   Porter, M. E. (1980). *Competitive strategy: Techniques for Analyzing Industries and Competitiors*. New York, USA: The Free Press.

78.   Porter, M. E. (1990). *La ventaja competitiva de las naciones [The competitive advantage of nations]*. Buenos Aires, Argentina: Vergara Editor.

79.   Porter, M., & Scott, S. (2001, Summer). Innovation: Location Matters. *MIT Sloan Management Review, 42*(4), 28.

80.   RAE. (2012). *Diccionario de la Real Academia Española [Dictionary of the Royal Spanish Academy]*, 22nd Edition. Retrieved November 5, 2014, from Mercadotecnia [Marketing]: http://lema.rae.es/drae/?val=mercadotecnia

81.   RAE. (2012). *Diccionario de la Real Academia Española [Dictionary of the Royal Spanish Academy]*, 22nd Edition. Retrieved October 31, 2014, from Innovación [Innovation]: http://lema.rae.es/drae/?val=innovación

82.   revistafortuna. (2013, February 20th). *http://revistafortuna.com.mx*. Retrieved from el tequila siempre nuestro [tequila always our]: http://revistafortuna.com.mx/contenido/2013/02/20/el-tequila-siempre-nuestro/

83.   Rodríguez Morales, L. (1989). *Para una teoría del diseño [For a design theory]*. Mexico City, Mexico: Tilde-UAM Azcapotzalco.

84.   Saínz de Vicuña Ancín, J. M. (2013). *El plan de marketing en la práctica [The marketing plan in practice]*. Madrid, Spain: ESIC.

85.   Santesmases, M., Sánchez, A., & Valderrey, F. (2003). *Mercadotecnia. Conceptos y estrategias [Marketing. Concepts and strategies]*. Mexico City: ITESM – Pirámide.

86.   Satué, E. (1988). *El diseño gráfico: desde los orígenes hasta nuestros días [Graphic design: from the origins to the present day]*. Madrid, Spain: Alianza.

87.   Schoell, W. F., & Guiltinan, J. P. (1991). *Mercadotecnia. Conceptos y prácticas modernas [Marketing. Modern concepts and practices]*. Mexico City: Prentice Hall Hispanoamericana.

88.   Schumpeter, J. A. (1978). *Teoría del desenvolvimiento económico [Theory of economic development]* (Fifth reprint ed.). Mexico City, Mexico: Fondo de Cultura Económica.

89.   Sobrino, R., & Mercado, F. (2006, January 15). Marketing Design. (A. Pérez Iragorri, Ed.) *a! Diseño*(77), 74-76. Retrieved March 20, 2007, from http://www.a.com.mx

90.   Stanton, W., Etzel, M., & Walker, B. (2007). *Fundamentos de*

Marketing [Fundamentals of Marketing] (13th ed.). Mexico City, Mexico: Mc Graw Hill-Interamericana.

91.   Taylor, J. W., & Shaw, T. R. (1990). *Mercadotecnia: un enfoque integrador [Marketing: an integrative approach]*. Mexico City, Mexico: Trillas.

92.   Telford, A. (2001, March-April). Diseño en México [Design in Mexico]. (C. &. Blanchard, Ed.) *Communication Arts, 43*(1), 115-130.

93.   Thompson, A., & Strickland, A. J. (1998). *Dirección y administración estratégicas: conceptos, casos y lecturas [Strategic Manaement: concepts, cases and readings]* (first edition ed.). Mexico City, Mexico: McGraw Hill.

94.   Thompson, A., & Strickland, A. J. (2004). *Strategic management. Concepts and cases.* USA: Mc Graw Hill.

95.   UL. (1973, March). Acquainted elements to fall down a swing. *University of London Newsletter*, 53.

96.   Wikipedia.org. (2015, January 13). *Competitividad [Competitiviness]*. Retrieved January 13, 2015 at 07:13, from Wikipedia, The Free Encyclopedia: http://es.wikipedia.org/wiki/Competitividad

97.   Wikipedia.org. (2015, February 13). *Diseño gráfico [Graphic Design]*. Retrieved February 13, 2015 at 15:07, from Wikipedia, The Free Encyclopedia: http://es.wikipedia.org/wiki/Diseño_gráfico

98.   Wikipedia.org. (2015, January 20). *Negocio [Business]*. Retrieved January 24, 2015 at 14:27, from Wikipedia, The Free Encyclopedia: http://es.wikipedia.org/wiki/Negocio

99.   Wikipedia.org. (2015, May 21). *Tequila Sunrise (cocktail)*. Retrieved from Wikipedia, The Free Encyclopedia: https://en.wikipedia.org/wiki/Tequila_Sunrise_(cocktail)

100.   Winfrey, O. (2014, April 28th). Oprah Winfrey on Career, Life and Leadership. Stanford, California, USA: Youtube. Retrieved from https://www.youtube.com/watch?v=6DlrqeWrczs

101.   Wingler, H. M. (1975). *Bauhaus. Weimar Dessau Berlin 1919-1933.* Barcelona, Spain: GG Diseño.

102.   Wong, W. (1995). *Fundamentos del diseño [Principles of form and design]*. Mexico City, Mexico: GG Diseño.

103.   Zimmermann, Y. (1998). *Del diseño [Of the design]*. Barcelona, Spain: GG Diseño.

About the author

I work as an independent, I design, write, produce music, and video for my own projects, from my place of residence in Merida, Yucatan. I have over 20 years of integrated design experience. At the same time being independent from 1999 to 2010, I have been a teacher in some educational institutions in Mexico City. I have a Bachelor of Graphic Design from *Universidad Nacional Autónoma de México* (*UNAM*) [National Autonomous University of Mexico]. Today I help people cope with the challenges with all phases to achieve success, from personal development to business. But I leading my activities with meditation and a healthy life, which I learn and practice to get the Sunrise from everywhere, only by joining its parties reach completely.

www.ingramcontent.com/pod-product-compliance
Lightning Source LLC
Chambersburg PA
CBHW070856180526
45168CB00005B/1837